HOW TO DEAL WITH ANGRY PEOPLE

For my wonderful children, Rhys and Tobin,

who make every day better.

Dr Ryan Martin

⚡ THE ANGER PROFESSOR ⚡

HOW TO DEAL WITH ANGRY PEOPLE

10 Strategies for Facing Anger
at Home, at Work and in the Street

How to Deal with Angry People

Ryan Martin

First published in the UK and USA in 2023 by
Watkins, an imprint of Watkins Media Limited
Unit 11, Shepperton House, 83–93 Shepperton Road
London N1 3DF

enquiries@watkinspublishing.com

1 2 3 4 5 6 7 8 9 10

Typeset by JCS Publishing Services Ltd
Printed in the United Kingdom by TJ Books Ltd

A CIP record for this book is available from the British Library

ISBN: 978-1-78678-664-7 (Paperback)
ISBN: 978-1-78678-727-9 (eBook)

www.watkinspublishing.com

CONTENTS

PRIORITIZING SAFETY

Please know that learning to deal with angry people is not about learning to tolerate physical and/or emotional abuse. You are under no obligation to stay in a relationship that is unhealthy for you, and if you ever feel you are in danger of harm, you should get to a safe place.

INTRODUCTION

Dealing with Angry People

The Moment I Knew We Were in Trouble

One afternoon in late 2021, I got an unexpected call that revealed how angry people out there really were. She was a librarian who told me she had heard about my work from a friend and was wondering if I might be able to train her staff on dealing with unruly customers.

"Can you tell me more about what's going on?" I asked.

"We're dealing with real problems from our clients," she responded. "Our staff has been overwhelmed by angry and even aggressive people, and we are trying to learn some strategies for how to deal with it." She went on to describe how her team was facing a lot of hostility from people coming to the library. She said she was hoping for strategies to help them depersonalize some of these interactions but also to help them de-escalate situations like these.

This was the moment I knew we were in trouble. I had already received a lot of media requests to talk about things like road rage, unruly people on flights, and school fights. We were still in the middle of the Covid-19 health crisis, being asked to wear masks in many public spaces and to physically distance when possible. These requirements were definitely leading to a lot of anger from people who didn't want to wear masks and/or didn't consider the pandemic a significant issue anymore. Accounts of flight attendants being yelled at or even punched* were widespread, so much so that the airlines were implementing

---

* This has actually happened more than once in the past two years. In one instance, a flight attendant had her nose broken after being punched twice by a passenger. In another, a flight attendant was punched multiple times and had several teeth chipped.

new policies and consequences in the hope of minimizing these instances of anger and aggression.

For some reason, though, this library situation seemed different to me. I've never once been mad at a librarian. Quite the opposite, in fact. My experiences with librarians have consistently been positive. I work with quite a few at the university and they are some of my best colleagues. When my kids were young, we would spend weekends at the library and never once had an issue. Frankly, and forgive me for stereotyping, but the librarians I've worked with strike me as some of the kindest and most helpful people around.

So when I got that call, my first thought was… yikes! How is it possible that we got to a place where people are yelling at librarians?[*] Now, I never want to rely on my own perceptions of things, so I decided to look and see if I was an outlier when it came to my position on the kindness of librarians. It turns out, no, I'm not. At least back in 2013[1], the vast majority of Americans had a fondness for the library – 94 per cent of people surveyed described the library as welcoming and friendly. Another 91 per cent said that "they personally have never had a negative experience using a public library." Honestly, an appreciation for libraries feels like one of the only things Americans agree on.

Taken together, one of three things is happening:

1. The tide has turned since 2013 and libraries have somehow become a source of great displeasure, leading to significant hostility toward librarians. I doubt this is what is going on.
2. The 6 per cent of Americans who don't see libraries as welcoming and friendly are the source of a lot of anger and aggression. I don't think it's this either.
3. There are a lot of people who see libraries as welcoming and friendly places, yet are still losing their cool when things don't go their way. I'm pretty sure it's this one.

---

[*] I asked a librarian friend of mine about this after the call and she said that, like any service-type job, she had to deal with angry patrons sometimes. She also told me that she had felt the same uptick in hostility as the person who called me.

Since then, these media and training requests related to dealing with angry people have become far more frequent. Service providers in particular, but people more generally, are telling me that they are at their wit's end when it comes to the hostility of others. Indeed, it does seem like we are in a particularly hostile time right now. While there's no international indicator of anger levels, we do have some data to suggest that people are particularly angry at the moment, at least in the United States. Reports of road rage are very high, including road-rage-related shootings[2], teachers across the United States are reporting more school violence[3], and service providers of all types are describing angrier customers and clients. Taken together, emotions are running hot right now and there don't seem to be any signs that people will cool off soon.

Two Types of Angry People

In our lives, we interact with angry people in two ways. There are those like above. These one-off interactions where a stranger becomes angry with us because of how we've done our job, how we are driving, or some other way they feel we are blocking their goals or treating them unfairly or poorly. This might be a customer at our place of business, a person we come across at a public event, or the person in the car behind us. We don't know their backstory or even what happened to them earlier that day. We don't know if they are usually angry and hostile or if we just bumped into them on an off day. All we know is that we're dealing with their rage in that moment, and we will likely never see them again once the interaction has ended.

The second way we deal with angry people, though, can be much more complicated. It's not a one-time meeting, but someone we interact with often, maybe even every day. Someone with an angry personality, who exists in our life in a way that we routinely come into contact with them. This could be our boss, our friend, a spouse, a sibling or parent, or even one of our kids.

These are not one-off interactions, but regular occurrences, and being able to interact, work, and live with them is critical to our success and happiness.

This book is designed to help you with both of these categories. For those of you who have to deal with a lot of angry people – whether it's because of your job (such as flight attendant, server, librarian) or some other reason – this book will provide you with valuable tools for getting through those one-off interactions successfully. For those of you who have a specific angry person in your life, this book will help you better understand them, work with them, and interact with them in a way that is productive, and also doesn't leave you suffering from their toxicity.

ANGER FACT

About a third of people say they have a close friend or family member who has an anger problem.[4]

Who This Book is For

This book is for anyone navigating the challenges of having an angry person or angry people in their life. This could include working in an environment where you routinely encounter angry people because of the nature of the job. Or it could include having a specific person you regularly interact with who has an anger problem. For instance:

- Does your romantic partner often lose their temper, snapping at you or others they interact with in a way that makes you uncomfortable?
- Are you the parent of a child or teen who routinely gets angry?

- Are you an adult child with a parent or parents who often snap, saying hurtful things or forcing you to walk on eggshells around them?
- Do you have a boss or co-worker who is quick to snap at you, leaving you feeling anxious at work?
- Do you have a close friend whose anger has proven to get in the way of your relationship with them?

Who This Book is Not For

This book is not for people who are in abusive relationships. It is not for people who are being regularly harmed, either physically or emotionally, by an angry person in their life. If you are in an abusive relationship, defined as "a pattern of behavior used by one partner to maintain power and control over another partner in an intimate relationship[5]," I would encourage you to set this book down and seek help from someone who can assist you in getting to safety. The National Domestic Violence Hotline, for instance, is a valuable resource in the US for anyone who may be in an abusive relationship. See the further reading and resources section at the end of the book for details of organizations in the US, UK, Australia, and New Zealand.

Now is a good time to point out a very important distinction that not everyone recognizes. There is a difference between *anger* and *aggression*. Anger is a feeling state. It's an emotion brought on by the belief that we are being treated unfairly or having our goals blocked. It's exceedingly common, with most people saying they experience it a few times a day to a few times a week.[6] It's different from the acts of harm that are sometimes associated with it. Those acts of harm reflect aggression, which is a behavior where a person intends to hurt a person verbally or physically.

This distinction is really important, especially in terms of this book. The world is full of angry people who aren't necessarily aggressive people. Anger can be expressed in near infinite ways and physical violence is a relatively rare consequence. People are far more likely to suffer other sorts of consequences such as feeling scared or sad after an angry outburst; they could get into a verbal altercation, damage property, drive dangerously, or use alcohol or other drugs. The angry people you interact with might not be abusive to you or anyone, but that doesn't make interacting with them easy. They can still have a very toxic influence on your life, leaving you feeling exhausted, overwhelmed, anxious, or even angry yourself.

Feeling Unprepared and Uncertain

I am a psychology professor who has been studying anger and other emotions for more than 20 years. I have conducted research on healthy and unhealthy expressions of anger, taught courses on anger and other emotions, and early in my career I did clinical work with angry clients. I have also made a point of connecting with people via my research and social media to better understand the lived experiences of both people who are angry and those who often have to live and work with angry people.

I decided to write this book after a TikTok series I did went viral. The series "How to Deal with Angry People" seemed to resonate so strongly with viewers that it felt like there was a real need for such information. I received thousands of comments and questions from people, and both Buzzfeed[7] and Bored Panda[8] did stories about the series. It was clear from their comments and questions that this was an area where people felt unprepared and uncertain. They asked thoughtful questions like: *How can we disengage if they won't leave us alone? What do we do when the angry person won't communicate with us? What if they aren't mad at us, but we're left dealing with their anger toward others?*

These and other similar questions really are interesting and thoughtful and nuanced, and I've used them to inform what I've included in this book. They've helped me better understand the situations people are dealing with and forced me to give some serious thought to how I can help people navigate these emotionally complicated interactions and relationship dynamics.

What these online conversations also revealed is how common it is for people to work with, live with, or otherwise interact with angry people. According to the British Association of Anger Management, about one-third of people have a close friend or loved one with an anger problem, but that likely doesn't capture the bulk of the problem because it ignores co-workers, regular customers, or even the person we may meet on the street on a random day. Anger problems appear to be increasing, so even if we aren't angry ourselves, we're still likely to come across such people regularly and often.

To prepare for writing this book, I interviewed quite a few people who either described themselves as angry or told me they had an angry person in their life (sometimes both). What was clear from these interviews was how often the angry person was intertwined into their life in a way that made separation from them difficult or even impossible. The angry person was a boss, a parent, a spouse, a former spouse and co-parent, or even one of their kids. They were people who had power over them (such as a boss or a parent) or people with deep personal connections (a spouse or a sibling) and the person I was talking with didn't feel like they could simply disengage from them. They felt trapped in this relationship with an angry person and didn't know how to deal with it.

Five Caveats

As you head into this book, there are five important things I want you to keep in mind. They are part of my worldview when it comes to understanding angry people, and really critical to getting the most out of this book.

Sometimes the Anger is Justified

Few people want to hear this, but sometimes the anger people have toward us is justified. We are human beings too, and thus capable of making mistakes. We do things, either intentionally or unintentionally, that cause problems for people. We may block their goals, treat them unfairly, or even treat them disrespectfully. Anger is not an inherently bad feeling state. In fact, it's a healthy and important emotion for people to feel, as it lets us know we've been wronged and provides us the energy we need to deal with that injustice. The anger this person is feeling toward us may be a reasonable and healthy reaction to something we did.

That does not mean, however, that their treatment of us is justified. Anger can be expressed in numerous ways, and some of those ways are cruel and unfair. We may find ourselves in a situation where we have done something wrong, another person is rightly angry with us, but is treating us in a way that is unacceptable. We can't work effectively with angry people unless we're fully willing to consider these dynamics. We have to be willing and capable of honesty, insight, and even some vulnerability. Acknowledging that we may have made a mistake and that we are partially culpable in any situation requires some emotional effort from ourselves, and we won't be successful unless we're willing to do just that.

TIP

Understand that you are under no obligation to stay in a relationship with an angry person when it is unhealthy or dangerous for you.

Anger Is Both a State and a Trait

I will have a lot more to say about this in the first chapter, but we need to acknowledge that anger can be both an emotional state and a personality trait. It is an emotional state in the sense that anyone can get angry in a particular moment. It's a normal and healthy emotional experience, much like sadness, fear, or happiness. At the same, though, there are some people who get angrier more often than others. When a person gets angry more often than most or when they experience that anger more intensely than others, we start to think of them as having an angry personality. For them, their anger is more of a trait than just a state. Their anger is part of who they are as a person.

We see the same dynamic with other emotions too. You have likely known someone who you consider to be relatively anxious. They feel fear and nervousness more than most people. That doesn't mean they are anxious all the time. It also doesn't mean that the non-anxious people in your life never get scared. They get anxious, nervous, and frightened too… just not as often. Sadness, happiness, pride, curiosity – they all exist as both emotional states and personality traits.

When People Are Angry With You, You Will Likely Respond with Your Own Complicated Set of Emotions

Other people's anger doesn't exist in an emotional vacuum. When people get angry at you, you likely feel things in response. You may, for instance, respond with your own anger (*how dare they treat me this way?*). You may get scared as your mind jumps to some possibly threatening outcomes. You may become embarrassed, ashamed, or even defensive as you think about your role in their anger.

More so than some other feeling states, anger can be considered a social emotion. It primarily occurs in social situations, so by definition there will be more than one set of emotions in any angering situation. Such a dynamic becomes far more complex and navigating such an experience requires a different level of emotional insight and understanding. We must be able to understand and manage our own emotions at the same time that we are understanding and managing theirs.

Angry People Aren't Necessarily Monsters

For various reasons, angry people are often seen as bad people. Anger is perceived as controllable in ways that sadness and anxiety are not, so people who have anger problems are thought of as culpable in ways that depressed or anxious people are not. Add to this that angry people might hurt those around them, through physical or verbal aggression, and there ends up being a particularly negative perception of people with anger problems. They are often considered thoughtless, selfish, insensitive, and cruel.

I want to push back on this perspective a little bit. Our anger can come from a lot of places, and not all of those places are rooted in cruelty or disrespect. Are there angry people who at their core are narcissistic or antisocial? Yes. Are there people whose anger is rooted in a deep-seated belief that they are better than others and who have a lack of remorse for others? Of course. Such people do indeed exist and their anger can be exceptionally toxic and potentially dangerous.

For others, though, their anger is rooted in something else. It may be hurt, fear, or even concern for the world around them[*]. There are people, for instance, with such strong opinions about justice that injustice of any sort is particularly triggering for them. They look around and see a world with deep unfairness, and they spend much of their life angry about it. Even small instances of unfairness send them into an anger spiral, not because of a lack of caring or understanding for others, but for the opposite reason. They care a great deal for humanity and can't stomach some of what they witness.

As you read this book, I'm going to ask you to do something that might be challenging. Please try to look at the angry people in your life through a lens of compassion and understanding. Make an effort to see the world through their eyes and to understand their origin story. This doesn't mean that you should

---

[*] People are sometimes surprised to learn that I put myself in this category. While I am unlikely to express my anger in a hostile or aggressive way, I find myself frequently angry about a variety of social issues.

put up with their hostility or tolerate their abuse. Far from it. I would never ask anyone to tolerate an abusive, hostile, or dangerous situation. It simply means that you make an effort to consider the world from their perspective and that you have concern for the ways they may have suffered.

TIP

Therapy services can be a useful step when distancing yourself from an angry person is challenging.

Sometimes, Though, Angry People May be Toxic and Dangerous

That said, we also need to recognize that some angry people may be bad for you. It's not necessarily that they are "bad people," rather their presence in your life may not be healthy for you. Much of what people have shared with me through the interviews I've done and through social media is that living with angry people, especially those who express their anger outwardly in aggressive ways, can be exhausting and take a considerable toll on one's mental health. They have told me that they spend much of their time not just managing their own emotions, but trying to manage the emotions of this angry person too. They never get to feel comfortable or be themselves because they are too busy trying to prevent this bomb from going off.

Please do not think of this book as a field guide for how to tolerate abuse. The last thing I want is for people to think that they are expected to endure hostile and aggressive behavior. In an ideal world, angry people would work on their own emotions so the rest of us wouldn't need to carry that emotional labor. They would deal with their own anger and they would treat people well. My last book, *Why We Get Mad: How to Use Your Anger for Positive Change*, was designed to help angry people do this very thing. The problem, though, is that not every angry person wants to be less angry. Their anger serves them in a way that they like. They might even be reinforced for their anger, so they would see changing that anger as harmful to themselves. Some other angry people, though, do want to change, but that change is scary and difficult. They recognize the harm they might be causing people and they want to do the work, but haven't found success yet.[*]

When the angry person in your life feels especially toxic to you, and when you see no other options, it is ok to draw some boundaries around your connections to them. This too can be hard for people to hear sometimes, but there is no rule that says you must keep people in your life. When interacting with particular people is unhealthy for you, you can keep it to a minimum or even eliminate it altogether.

Organization of the Book

Part One is about understanding angry people. I dig into the research on personality types, biology, emotional development, emotional contagion, and thinking styles. I see this as an important element of developing that compassion and understanding that is necessary but not sufficient when it comes to dealing with angry people. Even though this part offers a broader look at the experiences of angry people, each chapter provides some useful practical ideas along the way and ends with an activity to help you better understand the angry people in your life.

Part Two offers ten specific strategies for how to deal with angry people in the moment:

---

[*]   I heard from more than one person that they found reading my last book personally challenging for this very reason. They told me they had started to see the harm they might be doing to themselves and others, and seeing that harm made introspection really scary for them.

1. How to work out what you really want.
2. How to stay calm and collected.
3. How to recognize anger in different forms.
4. How to understand anger from the other person's perspective.
5. How to recognize when their anger is justified.
6. How to deal with those who won't communicate.
7. How to work productively with internet anger.
8. How to avoid character assaults.
9. How to know when to disengage.
10. How to combine strategies.

Throughout, I'll offer real-life examples from people I've talked to and share current research to help you navigate these emotionally taxing moments.

More importantly, though, this book will show you how to build and embrace an identity as someone who wants and is able to interact with angry people productively and effectively. It takes more than just tools to be successful in navigating the anger and hostility of others. Those tools are important, of course. You need to have them and you need to be able to use them. Beyond that, though, you need to have healthy outcomes in mind and you need to be able to stick to those goals as things get heated. This book will show you how to keep those goals in mind and embrace an identity as a calm and confident navigator of other people's anger.

PART ONE

UNDERSTANDING ANGRY PEOPLE

CHAPTER I

AN ANGRY PERSON OR A PERSON WHO IS ANGRY?

Anger Can Be Two Things

Anger can be an emotion – a feeling state – that we are all capable of experiencing. In this case, anger can be described as the psychological reaction to injustice, poor treatment, or having our goals blocked. It's an emotional desire to strike out at the person who wronged you or at the thing getting in your way. Like any emotion, it is associated with a relatively specific set of thoughts, physiological experiences, and behaviors.

At the same time, though, anger can be thought of as a personality trait. Here, we're describing a relatively consistent pattern of angry feelings, thoughts, and behaviors. Someone with an angry personality tends to get mad more often than most people, not necessarily because they encounter more provocations, but because they find things provoking that others do not. Like any personality trait, it isn't 100 per cent consistent. Just as anxious people are capable of moments without fear or nervousness, angry people are capable of moments without rage.

Case Study: Izzy – "Who he is as an angry person and who he is when he's not angry are very different"

I spoke with a woman named Izzy* who I met through social media. She reached out in response to a post where I asked for

---

* Not her real name. I asked everyone I spoke with to use fake names for these interviews. Most of the time they picked the name. Sometimes they asked me to choose, which really felt like a lot of pressure. I started thinking,

people who considered themselves angry or who had experience with an angry person. My short conversation with her revealed her to be a deeply insightful person, understanding her motivations and the motivations of those around her. She had a background in psychology, which was of course where much of this insight came from, but I got the sense that, separate from that training and education, she was just an introspective and emotionally wise person who thought a lot about why people, including herself, felt the way they felt and did the things they did.

Izzy grew up with an angry dad. She described him as having "struggled with anger for maybe all of his life." Before we get to that, though, let's talk about what he was like when he wasn't angry. Because her dad provides us with one of those cases where there was a real disconnect between who he was most of the time and who he was when he was mad. "Outside of his anger, he's generally a pleasant person to be around," Izzy explained. "He's charismatic and really loves talking to people. He is a very loving person."

At the same time, though, she said, "When he does get angry, he loses control emotionally. He'll lash out at people verbally. He'll say things that don't really seem aligned to the character he has when he's not angry." He would say things that were deeply hurtful. In fact, she said "he knows the thing to say that would be hurtful" in a given moment and will use that against people. For instance, one time when she disagreed with him, he got angry and responded with, "you're such a difficult person. I feel bad for whoever marries you."

When she was growing up, she thought she was the cause of his anger because he would blow up if she did something he didn't like. Now she has realized that "his anger comes from a place of not being able to manage feelings that are overwhelming to him." She thinks he gets anxious, stressed out, and disappointed easily and has a hard time regulating his emotions in these

"What if I pick a name they hate?" or "What if I pick a name that reminds them of someone from their past?"

situations. "If things feel out of control to him, that's really what triggers his anger."

His anger was typically directed at people he knew well, such as family. He wouldn't usually direct it at his co-workers or at strangers. Though she acknowledged that he was a little bit prone to road rage. Overall, though, "it would take more for him to get upset at a stranger than it would his family." She thinks this is because he feels comfortable with family so it's safer to express those feelings. The road-rage exception here is pretty good evidence that his safety plays a role here. As long as you keep your anger in the car and don't express it to the other drivers, it's a relatively safe place to get mad.

At the heart of this, it seems his anger comes from a place of insecurity. This was illustrated in the way he would become locked into a position. She said there was no way to change his mind when he was angry. They would never go back and talk about the situation that led to the anger either. Though, she said, "I think he would feel bad. Maybe he didn't recognize that he was wrong, but he did recognize how big a reaction he had." He would never say he was sorry. In fact, she said she could only remember hearing him say he was sorry a couple of times in her life. Instead, he would sort of pretend it didn't happen, and then he might go out and buy her something as an apology (like a treat or something she had said she wanted). She saw these as strategies for avoiding conflict.

One of the things she told me that was really interesting, and speaks to the role insecurity plays here, is that he makes a lot of assumptions about how she was perceiving him when there's conflict. She said he would say things like, "you think I'm such a horrible person or you think I'm stupid." These were things she wasn't thinking, but he would jump to these conclusions in a way that exacerbated his insecurity and defensiveness.

Izzy shared a lot about the impact of all this on her. She described how the patterns she experienced with him were built into later relationships. "When he gets really angry, there's nothing that will change his mind," she said. "If I disagreed with him or if I didn't want something or if I was trying to explain that he was hurting me in some kind of way, there was no getting through to him." She stopped trying to get through to him because it was ineffective. As an adult, though, she realized that when people were doing things she didn't like, she would get really angry because she assumed there was nothing she could do. Essentially, his anger taught her to feel helpless in relationships.

There were other long-term effects, especially tied to relationship dynamics, that played out for Izzy. She described how hard emotional vulnerability was for her because she learned from him that emotions were manipulative. When she would cry, he would accuse her of being manipulative to make him out to be the bad guy. Now, she thinks he probably felt ashamed and pushed that shame away by finding a way to blame her. At the same time, though, she gets anxious when she cries now because she's worried people will think she's lying or just trying to manipulate them. Plus, anger was what he used to control the people around him and she doesn't want to be that way. She often feels like she ends up managing other people's emotions in ways that feel a little bit "mothering" to her. In the end, much of this is rooted in the fact that she finds intense anger especially scary. "I still don't have a healthy relationship with anger," she told me.

Izzy told me that her dad has softened a little as he has gotten older. It's hard to tell if this due to the typical pattern of development or if it's more specific to how their relationship as evolved. As people age, they often tend to relax a little as it becomes more important to experience positive emotions. When Izzy moved away from home, their relationship changed quite a bit. They saw each other less, obviously, and that impacted the way anger played out in their relationship. But, she also thinks that he's become "more reflective" about his anger as he's gotten older and this has changed how he emotes.

Anger as an Emotion

Izzy's dad nicely illustrates how anger can be two things. An often sweet and loving person, he would get angry and "lose control emotionally," as she described it. Like a lot of people when they are angry, he would lash out in these circumstances. As I said earlier, the angry experience is associated with a particular set of thoughts, physiological experiences, and behaviors. When we get mad, for example, our thoughts often shift to those of blaming, judgement, and revenge. *How dare they, they should not have done that*, or even *I'll get back at them for this* are all things we might think when we get angry.

Similarly, we often lash out physically or verbally when we get angry. Those thoughts of revenge we might experience can lead to vengeful actions. Like with Izzy's dad, people will yell or say hurtful things. They will push, hit, or find other ways to aggress against the people they believed wronged them. Even when they don't actually behave aggressively, they may want to. Psychologists call these *action tendencies* – when we *want* to carry out a particular behavior as part of our emotional response, but, because we are human and have the capacity for impulse control, we can stop ourselves and direct our anger differently.

Finally, our anger brings with it a particular set of physiological responses. When we get angry, our fight-or-flight response kicks in to help prepare us to respond to the injustice or work through the blocked goals. Our heart rate increases, we start to breath more heavily, our muscles tense up, and our digestive system slows down. This fascinating and complex set of responses is rooted in our evolutionary history. Such responses offered our ancestors, human and nonhuman, a survival benefit. Their anger allowed them to respond with more energy and made it more likely that they would survive hostile altercations.

I'm guessing most of you can easily pull up a recent example of a time you got angry. Maybe it was over a mild inconvenience at the grocery store that slowed you down. Or maybe it was when you experienced a much more significant injustice that left you feeling disrespected and helpless. Regardless, that anger wasn't just normal, it was likely healthy. The anger we feel when we are treated badly or slowed down both alerts us to the poor treatment and energizes us to respond to the poor treatment.

TIP

One way to judge the healthiness of your anger is to pay attention to the consequences. Is your anger harming your relationships, leading to arguments or fights, or leading to other negative outcomes?

It's worth noting, though, that even though our anger is often good for us, it can still cause problems. It can disrupt our lives in significant ways when we don't manage it properly, when we get angry too often, or even when we get angry over the wrong things or at the wrong times. Learning to navigate our anger is an important part of being an emotionally healthy person.

It is also worth noting that some people get angry more often than others, express their anger in more aggressive and hostile ways, and suffer more frequent negative consequences as a result of their anger. Such people can be described as having an angry personality.

ANGER FACT

Almost a third of people surveyed described themselves as having an anger problem.[9]

What's a Personality Trait?

When psychologists talk about this dynamic – where an emotion is both a feeling and a personality characteristic – we refer to it as state–trait theory. Anger as an emotion is a *state*. Anger as a personality characteristic is a *trait*. A personality trait can be defined as a relatively consistent way of behaving, thinking, and feeling. If you were to describe a person as friendly, you likely mean that *most of the time* they treat people kindly and are pleasant to be around. When you describe a person as arrogant, you likely mean that they *often* show an exaggerated sense of their own importance. In both of these cases, though, the people in question *can* behave differently – a kind person can be cruel sometimes and an arrogant person can show vulnerability. Having a personality trait doesn't mean you are that way *all of the time*. It just means you are that way *much of the time*.

Trait theory originates with the work of Dr. Gordon Allport, one of the first psychologists to study and theorize on the personality. In one of his earliest publications[10], co-written with his brother*, they described some of the core traits that make up the personality including intelligence, temperament (which includes emotionality), self-expression, and sociability. A few years later, in 1936, Allport and Henry Odbert[11] provided a more detailed explanation of personality, defining traits as "generalized and personalized determining tendencies"† and using examples such as aggressive, introverted, and sociable. To illustrate the difference between a trait and a state, they go on to say, "All people are anxious on occasion… But *some* individuals suffer from an 'anxiety neurosis'… They are recurrently and characteristically anxious."

---

* I want to quickly note that Floyd, the older brother, is the first author on this paper, suggesting he did the majority of the work. While the rational part of my brain believes this to be true – that Floyd Allport really did write most of the paper – the younger sibling in me thinks Gordon did all the work and Floyd just threatened him with a wedgie or made him eat his socks until he let him be first author.

† Wow, doesn't that definition just flow right off the tongue? I literally couldn't make that sound more jargony if I tried.

If you were to replace the word "anxiety" with the word "anger" in this explanation, you would essentially get a description of what I'm talking about here. All people are angry on occasion, but some people suffer from more frequent, intense, and maladaptive anger. They are *recurrently and characteristically* angry.

It wasn't until 1961[12], though, that Allport wrote what is considered by many to be his most important work on the subject of personality traits, *Pattern and Growth in Personality**. Technically, it is a revision of his 1937 book of the same name, but it is a rather significant revision (which makes sense given how long had passed and how much new information there was in the field of psychology). It is here where he describes three different types of traits, writing "in every personality there are p.d.'s [personality dispositions] of major significance and p.d.'s of minor significance" (p. 365). He describes these dispositions of major and minor significance as cardinal, central, and secondary.

Cardinal traits are those characteristics at the core of *some* people's personalities. This is a dominant trait that essentially drives who someone is and what they do day in and day out. As Allport put it, "almost every act seems traceable to its influence." For some, a cardinal trait might be greed. Their behavior, thoughts, and feelings might be driven largely or even exclusively by the goal of making money or increasing possessions. For others, a cardinal trait might be honesty. They are motivated largely by a need to be truthful to those around them. So imagine these two people (one with a cardinal trait of greed and another with a cardinal trait of honesty) are in the same situation where they could stand to make a lot of money, but they would have to lie to do so. It is easy to know what each of them would do based on these cardinal traits.

---

* The book is dedicated "to my students," which I found to be a particularly sweet and nice reminder that these extraordinary scholars from the past were not just researchers and authors. They were also teachers.

We don't all have cardinal traits, though. In fact, Allport described them as unusual. We do, however, all have central traits. Allport described these as "those that we mention in writing a careful letter of recommendation*." Central traits are our primary personality traits. Those qualities that regularly influence our behavior and thoughts (such as intelligence, kindness, conscientiousness, introversion). These are relatively stable traits and central to how people see you and describe your personality. When you set up your friend on a date, you might say, "You'll like them. They are really...." Whatever you end that sentence with – funny, kind, smart, charming – is likely an example of a central trait. So when Izzy described her dad as an angry person, she was saying that one of his central traits was his anger. It doesn't mean he is *always* that thing. It simply means he is *usually* that thing.

Finally, secondary traits are those traits that tend to emerge only in particular types of situations. He described these as "less conspicuous, less generalized, less consistent, and less often called into play." For instance, I tend to be a rather laid-back driver who doesn't get too angry when I'm behind the wheel. That said, there is a specific circumstance when I find myself getting very frustrated. It's when I am running low on gas. I can tell you exactly what happens in these situations. I become preoccupied with the idea that I'm going to run out of gas and so I catastrophize every slight delay. The red light, the person driving too slowly, the traffic… they all become reasons why I am going to run out of gas, be stranded on the side of the road, and have my day ruined.† This is an example of a secondary trait. It's a personality characteristic in that it predicts my feelings and behavior, but only emerges in a very specific situation.

---

* Again, reminding me that he's a teacher and that writing recommendation letters has *always* been a thing academics have to/get to do.

† I once told this story as part of a free speaking engagement I was doing for a local group in Green Bay, Wisconsin. A week later, I was mailed a thank-you note for the talk that included… a gift card for gas. It was honestly one of the most thoughtful thank-you gifts I've ever received.

TIP

If you recognize that anger, either yours or someone else's, comes out during specific situations, try managing those situations. Prepare for them, modify them, or even avoid them.

This last type of trait is really tricky because it speaks to a fundamental question about personality. How can it be stable on the one hand *and* emerge in particular circumstances? Isn't that evidence that it's not really the trait influencing our behavior, but actually the situations we're in? If people only get mad in particular circumstances, it's hard to argue that it's their personality leading to the anger. It must be those particular circumstances leading to the anger.

The "Person vs. Situation Controversy"

In the late 1960s and 1970s, as one group of psychologists – the personality theorists – were trying to articulate these building blocks of personality, another group of psychologists, led by Dr. Walter Mischel, were arguing that the personality does not exist. On the surface, this claim might feel a little outrageous. How could the personality not exist? Don't we see proof of the personality all the time through our interactions with people?

Mischel's position, though, is relatively simple and straightforward, and, honestly, hard to argue with. In his 1968 book, *Personality and Assessment,* Mischel argued that the body of research shows a very low correlation between personality traits and behavior. More specifically, he pointed out that people don't typically behave consistently across situations. How someone acts at a party is different than how they act at work or at a movie. If a person's behavior changes so dramatically from situation to situation, then it was not their personality influencing their behavior. It was the situation.

This would be a really short book if I believed there was no such thing as a personality, so let's dig into how personality psychologists have responded to the idea that our environment matters more than our personality. In 1987, Dr. David Buss wrote an article titled "Selection, evocation, and manipulation"[13] where he outlined how personality influences and environmental influences on behavior can coexist. Specifically, he listed three "key mechanisms by which personality and social processes are intrinsically linked." I bet you can figure out what those three things are based on context clues in the name of the article, but in case not, they are: selection, evocation, and manipulation. Here's how each of them works.

Selection
We select many of the situations we find ourselves in and that selection is based, in part, on our personalities. We can think of situation-selection in terms of small things (should I go to this party on Saturday, should I watch the news this evening) or we can think of it in terms of more significant decisions (should I take this job, should I move to this city). An introverted person would be unlikely to go to the party or take a job in event planning, essentially *selecting out* of those situations. A conscientious person might choose to spend a Saturday afternoon paying their bills instead of socializing or might select a job that requires more detail-oriented tasks (such as editor).

How might situation-selection play out in terms of anger? Well, an angry person may unintentionally or intentionally select *into* situations that lead to anger. They may watch a political news show, engage in arguments over social media, or even watch sports that tend to lead to anger. It is unlikely that in most of these cases the person is selecting into these activities because the *want* to feel angry. They are likely doing it because they enjoy the activity or believe that engaging in the activity is important for them to do. Regardless of the intent, though, consistently selecting into activities that lead to anger is a sign of an angry personality.

Manipulation

We don't just select the situations we enter, we manipulate them. We make intentional decisions about how we enter those situations and how we interact with the other people involved. For instance, when a student enrolls in a course in college, it is situation-selection. They are deciding to enter a particular type of situation. But, they also likely make a number of decisions about *how* they participate in the course. They decide where in the room they sit and how they take notes. They may introduce themselves to the instructor on the first day, hoping to set a good first impression and manipulate* how the instructor perceives them throughout the course. They may even encourage a friend to take the course with them, again changing their experience with the situation. It's no longer the same experience it originally was or could have been because they have modified it.

For an angry person, this manipulation might look a few different ways. Their anger might lead to them manipulating situations in a way that is harmful or controlling of others. They may expect for a situation to go so poorly that they try to control people in advance. The angry co-worker might send assertive or even aggressive emails in advance of a meeting, doing something they don't want them to do (maybe even something they were not planning on doing). Alternatively, they may use their anger to manipulate people as Izzy's dad did. When things felt out of control to him, his anger served to keep other people in line. Angry people manipulate others, intentionally or unintentionally, by scaring them into behaving the way they want them to.

---

* The word "manipulation" has undeservedly negative connotations. People often describe others as manipulative in a negative way. Ultimately, though, there's nothing inherently wrong with trying to change the world around us. In fact, I would argue that all human behavior is manipulative. Everything we do is designed to influence the world around us. The more important question is: "Are we manipulating people in a way that is bad or harmful for them?"

Evocation

Finally, evocation is a little more complicated. Human beings, usually unintentionally, evoke responses from people through their interactions with them. The way people approach situations and the way they approach other people might encourage people to respond to them in particular ways. An outgoing person approaches interactions with strangers in a friendly and outgoing way. Consequently, the people they interact with have a tendency to mirror that style and respond in a similarly positive way. By being friendly, they are evoking friendliness from others.

Meanwhile, though, an angry person may unintentionally evoke unfriendliness from people. They may even evoke provocations from them. For instance, an angry person may go into a situation (a family get-together, a trip to the post office) anticipating a frustrating experience. That anticipation of frustration might lead them to approach the situation with impatience, a disrespectful tone, or just a general terseness. That impatience might evoke the same sort of rudeness and terseness in response so they are essentially creating the kind of provocation they were anticipating. It becomes a self-fulfilling prophecy.

What Kind of Personality Trait is Anger?

So, if anger is a trait, what kind of trait is it? It's hard to imagine anger being a cardinal trait for anyone. Remember, not everyone has a cardinal trait. In fact, according to Allport, they are quite rare. These are those traits that influence just about every behavior a person engages in or thought they have, and it's unlikely that someone could be such an angry person that their anger is the central part of their personality, influencing almost everything they do.

Most people I have talked to about this are like Izzy, describing the angry people in their lives as not angry *all the time,* but *quick to* anger when provoked. This would make anger more of a central or secondary trait. In this case anger is a central part of who they are, influencing much of what they do and think. Anger is not the only part of their personality, but it's a primary building block of who they are. To put it another way, we often think of kindness, assertiveness, or affability as personality traits – central or secondary – so why wouldn't we think of angriness that way?

There is actually really solid evidence for considering emotionality as a personality trait, and it can be found in what psychologists refer to as the Big Five Personality Traits. A full history of the Big Five is well beyond the scope of this book*, but the quick version is that, following Allport and Odbert's 1936 work, many scholars began working on identifying the primary personality traits using various statistical methods. Dr. Raymond Cattell was able to identify 16 traits in 1949[14] when he developed the Sixteen Personality Factor Questionnaire (the 16PF), but others followed that up to suggest just five primary traits. Most notable was the work of Drs. Paul Costa and Robert McCrae who developed the NEO-Personality Inventory (NEO-PI)† in 1985[15].

What emerged from this analysis were the following five personality traits: openness, conscientiousness, extraversion, agreeableness, and neuroticism. This last one, neuroticism, is really a combination of emotion-related qualities. People who are neurotic tend to be emotional, temperamental, and anxious. They are quick to feel things, including fear, guilt, sadness, and anger. So, according to Costa and McCrae, emotionality is not just a personality trait, but one of the five most relevant personality traits.

---

* Some scholars date the history of these traits back to Hippocrates, but the more modern roots of the Big Five can be found in that 1936 article by Allport and Odbert. So those are your choices. Either 90 years ago or 2,400 years ago.

† Interestingly, they first identified three personality traits: Neuroticism, Extroversion, and Openness (NEO) and published the first version of the scale based on that in 1976. That's why the scale is called the NEO-PI.

The Angry Personality

In 1996, Dr. Jerry Deffenbacher, along with seven other researchers from Colorado State University, wrote an very important work[16] on the subject of the angry personality. While eight authors is a lot of authors for a research paper, this particular paper was completed over the course of eight years, tested five different hypotheses related to the angry personality, and included eight different research projects within it. It is an extensive series of projects that remains a defining work in understanding anger as a personality trait.

To break it down quickly, the researchers had five hypotheses that all served a single goal – to establish that anger really could be considered a personality trait. To do all this, they ran eight separate research projects using a variety of questionnaires that measure different aspects of anger. In one of these eight studies, for instance, they looked at people with unusually high or low scores on a test of trait anger (a measure of anger as a personality trait). Those participants came in for a session where they were asked to complete a number of short activities (take additional questionnaires, provide blood pressure and heart-rate data, listen to a provoking situation). Participants who had scored high on this test were more likely to become angry in response to the provocation, were more likely to experience anger on a day-to-day basis, and experienced more intense physiological symptoms (such as increased heart rate and blood pressure).

Later in this same paper, the researchers established that people who scored high on the scale suffered more serious anger-related negative consequences. They were more likely to hurt someone as a result of their anger, to break something when angry, or to use drugs or alcohol when angry. In fact, they asked these angry participants to describe the two worst anger incidents in the past year. The researchers coded the responses and found that those who had scored high on this test of their angry personality suffered the most severe consequences.

What makes this paper so important both to the overall field of anger and to the premise of this book is that it establishes something really important about anger: That we can consider it a personality trait as well as an emotion. As described by Deffenbacher and his colleagues, "trait anger is a fundamental individual difference in the propensity to become angry." People with this personality trait are more likely to get angry, experience anger more intensely, express their anger in more maladaptive ways, and experience more negative consequences.

Angry People Can Look All Kinds of Ways

What is important to remember about anger as a personality trait is that it does not always look as you might expect. For most, when they think about angry people, they think about someone like Izzy's dad. Someone who yells or says hurtful things. Someone who is controlling and treats people badly. Someone who is uncomfortable to be around because you cannot always predict what will set them off. Frankly, even the descriptions used by Deffenbacher and his co-authors feel like a somewhat narrow view of an angry personality.

Anger can be expressed in many ways. While some angry people yell and scream, others pout or withdraw. Others express their anger in more passive-aggressive ways by spreading rumors or intentionally failing to meet their responsibilities. Anger can be expressed in all sorts of positive ways too, but since this book is about dealing with more toxic forms of anger, we're going to focus on these negative expressions.

ACTIVITY: UNDERSTANDING THE ANGRY PERSON IN YOUR LIFE

Presumably, you've chosen to read this book for one of two reasons: (1) the nature of your work requires that you encounter angry people relatively regularly or (2) there is a specific angry person in your life that you are trying to learn to work more effectively with. If it's the latter, I would like you to take some time to think about what their angry personality is like. Answer the following questions about them.

1. Which kind of trait do you see their anger as: cardinal, central, or secondary?
2. Can you recognize situations where they might intentionally or unintentionally select, manipulate, or evoke provocations from their environment?
3. How do they tend to express their anger and what are some of the consequences of that expression style?

Why Are They Angry?

Whether the angry people you deal with are aggressive, toxic, or just sort of irritating, you need to have tools in place that will allow you to effectively deal with them. One of those tools is a thorough understanding of *why* they are angry. By this, I don't mean the specific circumstances that led to a particularly angry incident (though that is important). I mean the broad elements of their upbringing, culture, genetics, and worldview that led to them being an angry person. Were they just born that way? Or is their anger the result of a complicated life history?

In the next chapter, we'll talk about the biology of anger. What are we born with and what do we learn along the way?

CHAPTER 2
THE BIOLOGY OF ANGRY PEOPLE

"As Indicated by Frequent Physical Fights or Assaults"

Every semester, in my psychopathology course, we spend about two weeks on personality disorders. Personality disorders are defined in the *Diagnostic and Statistical Manual of Mental Disorders* (DSM-5-TR[17])[*] as "an enduring pattern of inner experience and behavior that deviates markedly from expectations of the individual's culture." Essentially, the implication here is that there is something wrong with the person's personality in a way that causes emotional, behavioral, and social problems. We see this pattern in the way people think, feel, and interact with others. Examples of personality disorders include narcissistic personality disorder, paranoid personality disorder, and antisocial personality disorder.

This last one, antisocial personality disorder, tends to jump out to students as particularly interesting. People with antisocial personality disorder have a habit of disregarding and violating the rights of others. They harm people both physically and verbally. They lie to people and exploit them for financial gain. They routinely get into physical fights and they often show very little remorse for any of these wrongdoings. For students this disorder is interesting because their minds often jump to topics of serial killing and other examples of violent offenders they've been

---

[*] The DSM, published by the American Psychiatric Association, is a 1,000-plus-page book describing all of the diagnosable mental health conditions. It lists everything from Major Depressive Disorder, Recurrent, with Psychotic Features to Anorexia Nervosa, Binge Eating/Purging Type to Non-Rapid Eye Movement Sleep Arousal Disorder, Sleepwalking Type, with Sleep Related Eating.

exposed to through the media.* This is, of course, fascinating to me too, but I'm more intrigued by this disorder because it's one of just a handful of places in the DSM where anger or a synonym for anger is listed as a symptom of a disorder.† In this case, it's "irritability and aggressiveness, as indicated by frequent physical fights or assaults."

What students inevitably want to talk about with this or any personality disorder (including borderline personality disorder, which is another place in the DSM that includes anger as a symptom) is what causes them. They want to know if a person is born antisocial or if it's a product of their upbringing and environment. It's a great question with an exceedingly complicated answer. These disorders, like many others, are pervasive and all encompassing. Essentially, the question students are asking is "What causes our personality?" and there isn't just one answer to that question.

Case Study: Nathan – "I don't want to be a tyrant"

A one-time client of mine, Nathan‡, was working with me to address his own anger problems. The pattern for him was fairly predictable. Most of the time, he wasn't an angry guy. In fact, he was relatively laid back. He was a successful college student at the time, had a lot of friends who seemed to like him and get

---

*   What many of them haven't realized yet is that violence isn't the only way to hurt people. There are all sorts of ways to take advantage of people that don't include aggression. A politician, CEO, or police officer who uses their position of power as a means of taking advantage of people may very well have antisocial personality disorder.

†   There's a long and complex explanation for why anger isn't thoroughly listed as its own disorder in the DSM that includes the document's roots in psychodynamic thinking, perceptions of anger as controllable compared with other emotions, and a fear of its use as an insanity defense. Regardless of the reasons, though, one of the consequences is angry people not getting care when they need it.

‡   Not his real name.

along with him, and he was always very pleasant in our therapy sessions. I never once saw him angry in our interactions.

The predictable pattern, though, was that he would go out on weekends with his girlfriend, get angry over something she did, and snap at her. He was never physically abusive to her, but he was undeniably verbally and emotionally abusive. He admitted all of this, telling me that he would yell at her, say cruel things to her, and yell at her friends when they tried to intervene. Sometimes alcohol was a catalyst here, but not always.

Even though I never saw him angry, I saw him sad and scared plenty of times. This was the other predictable part of the pattern. He would experience intense guilt, sadness, and shame after these incidents. This young guy who was such a villain to his girlfriend and her friends would be a puddle in my office, sobbing over what he had done and said.* He would tell me how much he hated all of this about himself, and that he just couldn't seem to stop himself in the moment. One day, through sobs and tears, he said "I don't want to be this way. I don't want to be a tyrant. I don't want people to be scared of me."

Nathan had grown up with a tyrant. His father was an angry person, but in a very different way than Nathan was. Nathan's anger was largely situational. To use Allport's terminology, it was a *secondary trait*. He got angry in a specific set of circumstances and it seemed to be rooted in jealousy and a desire to control his girlfriend. He was scared of losing her and that fear came out in a really awful way. Nathan's dad, though, wanted to control everything and everyone. He was quick to snap, not just at Nathan, but at anyone he interacted with. For Nathan's dad, the anger was a *central trait*.

His anger was wildly unpredictable. You could essentially count on it to be two things: frequent and intense. Otherwise, Nathan had a hard time knowing when or why that anger would come up. He would encounter a situation he didn't like and he

---

* I fully realize that this is a common pattern in abusive relationships, by the way, and this is not an attempt to minimize or justify the pain and suffering he had undoubtedly caused his girlfriend. I'm just painting a full picture for you.

would get angry about it. He also tended to voice that anger in a way that was really scary to Nathan. He would yell and he would swear. Sometimes at Nathan, his siblings, or Nathan's mom, but often just at strangers.

Nathan told me that he spent his entire life scared of his dad. Whenever they were together, he was worried his dad would snap – maybe at him or maybe at someone else around them. He told me that both of those things were scary to him. He hated the sound of his dad yelling, even when it wasn't at him. He spent his life on eggshells* anxious that he would do something that made his dad angry.

Worse yet, he would worry that someone around him would do something to make his dad angry. It was an odd fear for him because he knew that he couldn't control what the people around him did, yet he spent quite a bit of time thinking about it. He would go to a restaurant with his dad and he would start to panic if it seemed like the waiter was taking too long, scared it would make his father angry. He would start to get anxious if one of his siblings was doing something that might frustrate his dad, worried his dad would yell at them.

He would take steps, then, to try and prevent anyone else from doing something that might make his dad angry. He would find himself impatient on behalf of his dad, hurrying the waiter along or trying to speed up the person walking too slowly in front of them. He knew his dad's frustrations and would try desperately to cut them off early or even before they started. He would scold his siblings for being too wild, try to change the subject when they hit a conversation topic his dad didn't like, and even avoided talking to his dad about personal things that he thought might set him off in some way.

It was from this dynamic that his need for control came about. The "misbehavior" of others angered his dad, and that anger scared Nathan. His mechanism for coping with his dad's anger

---

* This is a refrain I have heard from just about everyone I talked to who lived with an outwardly angry person. They talked about how exhausting it was, and many used the expression, "walking on eggshells."

was to try and prevent it, and sometimes that meant trying to control the people around him. His current girlfriend (and as we later learned, a lot of other people in his life) were bearing the brunt of that. He wanted people to behave in a particular way. He became anxious and frustrated when they didn't do what he expected or wanted, and so he was unintentionally trying to keep people around him "in line." Sometimes, like with his girlfriend, he used his own anger to maintain that control.

So we get how Nathan became so controlling, but how did Nathan's dad get so angry? A deep dive into his personality, at least from Nathan's perspective, revealed that his anger stemmed from a lot of different traits that made him more likely to get angry throughout the day and more likely to express that anger outwardly. He was, for instance, impatient. He wanted things accomplished quickly and correctly. He was also prone to judgement. He had high expectations of those around him and when they failed to meet those expectations, he was very critical of them. Finally, he did not hesitate to tell people what he thought of them. He was very vocal in his criticism and this led to his often loud and aggressive outward expressions of anger.

TIP

Try to notice some of the complicated factors that might be informing a person's angry personality. Is it driven by impatience, a need for control, entitlement, or some other factor?

G by E Interactions

Nathan's story is an interesting one because we can see some evidence of two different ways that anger was passed on from his dad to him: genetics and upbringing. He was influenced by his father in a variety of ways, some of which started before he was even born. Any conversation about genetics and anger (or genetics and anything really) needs to start with the fact that we can't really separate our genes from the environment. They simply can't be disentangled from each other. As it is often compared to, it would be like baking a cake and asking what made it taste good, the sugar or the flour. Even though they were separate to begin with, once you mixed them together they interacted to make the cake what it is. If you take either of them away, it's just not the same cake. In the case of Nathan, you can't really say that his anger problems were the result of his genetics or his upbringing. Rather, his anger problems were the result of both. This is what scientists call the "gene by environment interaction" or if you want to sound hip and cool, the "G × E interaction" (G by E).

The G × E interaction* means that our characteristics, personality and otherwise, are influenced by an interchange between our genes and our environment. We may start our lives with a predisposition to some characteristic (anxiety, intelligence, anger) but that predisposition is subject to the environment we develop in. To use an obvious example, a person may be born with a genetic predisposition to be smart (at least as defined in the narrow way we tend to define intelligence). If that person, though, is exposed to environmental toxins (such as lead, mercury, alcohol) *in utero* or early on in life, that potential for high intelligence will likely be stunted. They will be unlikely to achieve the high IQ they were predisposed to obtain based purely on their genetic makeup.

While that is a dramatic example, the same sort of phenomenon occurs with any characteristic. We inherit a genetic predisposition to be short or tall and that predisposition is influenced by our diet or other contributing factors. We may

---

* See how "hip and cool" I sound.

not end up being as short or tall as was expected based on our genes. We may inherit a predisposition for anxiety but our life experiences, especially when young, will mitigate that and we may never develop the anxious personality we were predisposed to. The opposite may happen as well. A person may have no significant genetic predisposition to anxiety, but early on is exposed to stressors or traumatic experiences that lead to the development of an anxious personality.

In fact, this G × E interaction is ultimately what geneticists actually study. They are not simply interested in the genes. To quote Dr. Francis S. Collins of the National Human Genome Research Institute:

> Lots of people assume that we geneticists are only really interested in the genes and we don't think the environment is very important. Well, that's certainly not the case. For most complex diseases like diabetes and cancer, or heart disease, it's an interchange between genes and environment that gives rise to disease. You may be predisposed in a certain way by genetics, but you're probably not going to get the disease unless the environmental trigger is present, too. So this is a hugely important area of current research, to try and understand how the genes and the environment work together and how we can modify the environment for somebody whose genetic susceptibilities indicate that they're at risk.[18]

The Genetics of Anger

What this means in terms of anger is that while there are known genetic predictors of anger and aggression, those genetic predictors *interact* with environmental forces to give rise to chronic anger. A person like Nathan might be born with a high potential for anger problems, yet may never actually develop those anger problems because their environment did not bring those problems out in a meaningful way. At the same time, a person with no significant genetic predisposition to anger could develop in an environment that leads to serious anger problems.

When it comes to antisocial personality disorder, there has been plenty of research exploring the genetics involved. That research was summed up beautifully in a 2010 project conducted by Dr. Christopher Ferguson who used an approach called a meta-analysis.[19] A meta-analysis is a type of study where you explore the combined implications of the already published research on a particular topic. In this particular study, Dr. Ferguson found 38 published articles that had studied antisocial personality disorder through twin, adoption, or behavioral genetics research designs.

Twin and/or adoption research can be a powerful way to explore genetic predispositions. With twin research, you can make comparisons between identical and fraternal twins to better understand heritability rates. If antisocial personality disorder, for instance, were 100 per cent genetic (it's not), when one identical twin had it the other one would too. But if one fraternal twin had it, the other twin would have it about 50 per cent of the time because fraternal twins share approximately 50 per cent of their genes on average (same as non-twin siblings). What makes this particularly interesting is because, when raised together, both identical and fraternal twins share very similar environments and upbringing (potentially even more so than non-twin siblings because they are the same age). So, the impact of the environment remains largely the same for both of them. The primary difference between them is their genetic background.

Adoption studies have a similar principle. When adopted kids share no genetic relationship to their adoptive parents, you can make comparisons between the children and both their adoptive and biological parents. You can explore which traits they have that are most similar to their biological parents (who they share their genes with) and which are most similar to their adoptive parents (who raised them and share a similar environment with them). When Dr. Ferguson looked at the near 40 studies that had used these methods to study antisocial personality disorder, his conclusion was that approximately half (56 per cent) of the variance in antisocial personality disorder could be explained by genetics.

This of course doesn't mean it's set at birth and there's nothing that can be done. Remember, there's an interplay between genetic and environmental factors. So what this really means is that people might inherit an increased likelihood to develop antisocial personality disorder. That predisposition then is subject to their upbringing, environmental exposures, peer relationships, educational opportunities, and a host of other factors.

The research on antisocial personality disorder is relevant here largely because anger plays an important role in this condition and there's been so much more research on this disorder than on anger specifically. We have far less information when it comes to the role of genetics on anger (especially compared to the research that's been done on other emotion-related experiences like anxiety and depression).[*] So what do we know about anger more specifically? Is the emotion itself or even how people express it genetic?

In 2005, Dr. Xiaoling Wang and colleagues designed a study to test just this.[20] They looked at the anger expression styles of 306 pairs of twins, both identical and fraternal, and found that there were indeed genetic contributors. This study wasn't trying to predict how often or how angry people got, but how they expressed it. What they found was that suppression (holding your anger in) and control (deep breathing, counting) were best predicted by genetic factors. Expressing your anger outwardly was best predicted by shared environmental influences. There's an interesting theory here as to why that would be – why some expression styles would be better predicted by genetics than others – but we're going to discuss it more in the next chapter when we talk about upbringing.

---

[*] This is likely one of the consequences of anger not being adequately found in the DSM-5-TR. As a general rule, things that are in the DSM receive far more attention and funding for research than things not in the DSM.

Anger and the Brain

How do these genetic predispositions actually influence our anger? What might our genes actually change in the brain or elsewhere to serve as the building blocks of an angry person? If Nathan did indeed inherit his dad's temper, how did it happen? It can be difficult or even impossible to identify the specific connections between genes and the emotional responses they might predict. In fact, when we talk about genetic predispositions, we're not talking about a single gene that causes anger (or anxiety, intelligence, or anything else). It's rarely, if ever, that simple. Instead, it's a combination of genes that might be associated with increases or decreases in the sizes of particular brain structures or hormones.

For instance, a 2013 study found that amygdala size was predicted by a combination of genes.[21] The amygdala comprises of two little matching structures deep in the center of the brain that are often described as emotional computers. When we get angry, it's because our amygdala has taken in information that it has deemed provoking. It then initiates an anger response. Consistent with the emotional computer metaphor, it processes information (usually from the outside world but also from our memories and even our imagination*) and launches emotional responses to that information. Essentially, the amygdala is the part of the brain that hits the "get mad" (or sad, or scared, and similar emotions) button in the brain. When this happens, it sends signals to other structures in the brain, and the dominos begin to fall as the angry response ensues.

---

* Never doubt the very real provoking nature of our memories. We can make ourselves mad all over again by just remembering a time we were provoked. So when I think back on some of those hostile social-media comments I have received, my heart rate actually increases, my muscles actually tense up, and I actually start to sweat.

ANGER FACT

Anger is often experienced with other emotions such as sadness, fear, guilt. One of the reasons for that is because the biological underpinnings of these emotional experiences are all very similar.

The next domino in the sequence is the hypothalamus which controls our autonomic nervous system and initiates our fight-or-flight response. Our heart rate increases, our breathing increases, our muscles tense up, we start to sweat, and our digestive system slows down. This is how our body prepares itself to flee (if you're scared) or to fight (if you're angry). It's part of a complex sequence that exists to energize you to flee from danger or confront injustice. Simultaneously, your amygdala sends messages to your facial motor nucleus, which is a cluster of neurons in the brain stem that control your automatic facial expressions. These are the expressions that happen immediately when you emote; the ones you don't have immediate control over (such as furrowed brow*, narrow lips, hard stare).

These are just the parts of the anger experience we have no (or minimal) control over. They are the parts that happen immediately in response to the provocation before we can start to exercise some management strategies. Deep breathing will, for instance, slow down that fight-or-flight response once it's started, and while we can retake control of our facial expressions intentionally, we can only do that after that initial response has happened. The part of our brain responsible for retaking

---

* I have a permanent crease in between my eyes which I'm convinced has less to do with anger and more to do with stress and focus. Regardless, it came up on social media recently and let's just say that I was psychologically unprepared for how many people were going to recommend Botox.

control – whether through deep breathing, initiating different facial expressions, or controlling our desire to lash out physically or verbally – is our prefrontal cortex. This is the area of the brain right behind the forehead that is involved in decision-making, planning, and other advanced thinking tasks. It is here where we decide what to do with that anger. It is here where some people can rein in that desire to lash out.

This too has been shown to be influenced at least in part by our genes. A 2007 paper, for example, that reviewed brain-imaging studies – meaning the authors reviewed a bunch of magnetic resonance imaging (MRI) research – found that genetics predicted the size of the prefrontal cortex.[22] Our ability to control our anger, to stop ourselves from lashing out, is explained by the activity of this part of our brain, which exists as it does because of the genetic material we inherited. But the structures of our brain are not the only thing we inherited that might influence our anger and aggression. The hormones we release that might influence our anger are also predicted by our genes.

The Complicated Impact of Testosterone

I'm going to proceed cautiously here because little makes me more nervous than talking about testosterone as it relates to anger and aggression. Given testosterone's relationship to biological sex, any discussion where it's implied that "testosterone causes aggression" ends up being interpreted by some as "testosterone is why men are more aggressive than women." The latter is not a fair description for a variety of reasons. First, there are lots of reasons why men tend to be more aggressive than women. Second, testosterone doesn't necessarily increase anger and aggression, at least not the way people think.

Here's what we know about testosterone, aggression, and anger. Testosterone is a sex hormone that plays a role in sexual maturation in both males and females. In puberty, testosterone is associated with the further development of the sex organs, muscle size, bone growth, and so on. In addition to these maturation effects, though, testosterone also has sexual activation effects in that it is released prior to and during sexual arousal. Historically, and with good reason, it has been thought to be a biological cause of aggression. What we've found more recently, though, is that this link is exceedingly muddy and likely not as strong as most people think.

Testosterone does seem to predict aggression, but with quite a few confounding factors along the way (meaning, it doesn't predict aggression on its own and it doesn't predict all types of aggression). Most of the research on this has been done with animals, and the consistent finding is that because testosterone is associated with the seeking of social status, it seems to better predict social forms of aggression.[23] For instance, it is a pretty good predictor of dominance or territorial aggression (physical violence that's motivated by a desire for power or property) in most mammals. It is not, though, as good a predictor of predatory aggression or defensive aggression in animals.

Most of the research on humans, especially until recently, has been correlational. Researchers have essentially measured participants' testosterone, mostly in men, and their history of violence and looked for relationships between the two. When they've done this, aggression has been linked to severity of crimes, including rape and murder, but unlinked to non-violent crimes like theft or drug abuse. On the surface that seems like pretty solid evidence that testosterone increases aggression. Whenever we do correlational research, though, there are questions about the directionality. Is the high testosterone level causing the violence or does the violence increase the testosterone level?[24*]

More recently, the increased use of testosterone replacement therapy has allowed some more thorough research of the impact

---

* The 1978 study by Jeffcoate and colleagues found exactly this. They confined five men to a boat for two weeks and monitored their testosterone each day. They also rated the men on aggressiveness each day, and they found that as the men established a hierarchy, their testosterone levels changed along with that hierarchy. They concluded that "under some circumstances social interaction may modify endocrine status in humans."

of testosterone on human anger and aggression. Researchers have been able to experimentally manipulate testosterone levels in such a way that they can assess the impact of that manipulation on emotion and behavior. For instance, in one recent study[25] researchers divided male participants into two groups, one that was given testosterone and another that was given a placebo, and had them play video games. What the participants did not know, however, was that the joystick they were using was intentionally defective. That meant that the participants could not win and get the reward they had been promised if they won.[*] They found that the group who had been given testosterone was no more aggressive than the other group, but this group was indeed angrier than that other group. This study is but one in a series of studies in the past 15 years to illustrate this interesting relationship, that exogenous testosterone seems to lead to increased anger, but not necessarily increased aggression.

It is likely that at least some of this testosterone-induced anger is rooted in testosterone's role in the desire for increased status. People who desire higher status are often angered when those desires are thwarted. It's a form of goal-blocking. They want to be recognized for their accomplishments (job status, athletic accomplishment, or even a video game victory like the study above) and they feel angry when they either don't achieve those goals or when they feel unrecognized. When they don't get what they think they deserve, including recognition, they get mad.

Taken together, what does all this mean? First, testosterone is associated with certain types of aggression in animals, but maybe not so much in humans. Second, testosterone is associated with status-seeking in both animals and humans. Third, experimental manipulations of testosterone demonstrate that it does cause angry responses to having one's goals blocked. Finally, status seeking is likely associated with anger in humans. Consequently,

---

[*] Adult-Ryan finds the defective joystick research design hilarious. He's played enough video games and been around enough people playing video games to know how frustrating this would be. Child/Teenage-Ryan, who loved video games and took them very seriously, finds this research design unconscionable.

the impact of testosterone on human anger and aggression is likely a combination of direct and indirect effects. High levels of testosterone increase the propensity for anger and aggression (direct) and high levels of testosterone lead to a desire for higher status, which increases the propensity for anger (indirect).

Getting back to what started this discussion – how genetics might influence our anger – testosterone is undeniably predicted by our genes. We've had research on this for quite some time, but in the past decade alone, multiple studies have demonstrated through a variety of different methods that our genes explain testosterone levels. One of these studies included data from more than 400,000 participants and showed that (1) testosterone levels are inherited for both men and women and (2) those high levels also predict a variety of physical health consequences.[26]

Of course, none of this matters unless it informs the way we think about the angry people in our lives so that we may deal more effectively with them. We can't intervene in another person's biology, so why is this important? For me, it goes back to something I brought up in the introduction – that we should try to approach the angry people in our lives from a place of compassion and understanding. To really understand the angry people we deal with, we need an understanding of where that anger comes from.

The "E" in "G × E"

As I was looking at the current research on genetics and testosterone, I found a recent study that gave me pause. It was a 2018 paper[27] that looked at both genetic factors and childhood environmental factors in the prediction of testosterone. The authors of the study, Dr. Kesson Magid and colleagues from Durham University, argue that testosterone levels were better predicted by childhood experiences than by genetics. It's a smaller study, only 359 participants compared to the 400,000-person study I describe above, so I am cautious about drawing too many conclusions from it. At the same time,

---

ACTIVITY:
WHAT DOES BIOLOGY HAVE TO DO WITH IT?

Regarding any angry people in your life, take some time to think about what might be the biological contributors to their angry personalities. In some cases you may have no idea. You may not know them well enough to have a clear sense of any genetic predispositions. But based on what you do know about their biological family history (or maybe their tendency toward impulsive behaviors that aren't anger related), answer the following questions about them:

1. To what degree do you think their anger was inherited?
2. Does the knowledge that their anger is likely, in part, the product of their genetic history provide any empathy?

---

though, it gets at the E part of the G × E interaction we've been talking about. All of these biological differences (such as genes, brain structures, hormones) we've been talking about as predictors of anger, they are absolutely rooted in our genes. At the same time, though, our experiences – particularly those in childhood – matter. Nathan wasn't just the product of his dad's genes. He was the product of his dad's parenting. His anger also came from his dad's behavior, his dad's worldview, and from dynamics of their relationship. In the next chapter, we'll talk more specifically about those developmental factors and how they influence anger.

CHAPTER 3

EMOTIONAL UPBRINGINGS

Learned Expressions

When my oldest son was three years old or so, my wife and I were having a heated conversation in our kitchen. I don't remember what it was about, but likely something related to politics. We weren't arguing. In fact, I'm pretty sure we agreed with one another, but we were both angry about the topic and the discussion was fairly intense. Our voices were raised, our faces were stern, and I was standing, as I often do when I'm angry or talking about something serious, with my right arm across my diaphragm, my left elbow resting on my right wrist, and my chin resting on my left hand.*

My son was in the room, and in the middle of the conversation I looked down at him and noticed that he was standing in the exact same way I was standing. He was looking up at me with a stern look on his face, his arm crossed in front of him, his elbow resting on his wrist, and his chin resting on his hand. It was both adorable and poignant for me. Both my children are adopted. I pass nothing on to them genetically speaking and we look nothing like each other physically. So seeing him resemble me in another way was really powerful. It was also a fascinating example and important reminder that much of what we pass on to our children, especially in terms of emotional development, is not rooted in our biology.

---

* Honestly, I'm not sure where I picked this up, but given the nature of this chapter, it would be interesting and fun to know where I learned it.

Case Study: Simone –
"So much of my childhood was feeling that nobody understood"

When I talked with Simone, she was a soon-to-be-40-year-old woman who described herself as "successful by most societal standards." She had a good job and was financially independent. She was unmarried and didn't have kids. She lived, as she described it, "joyfully alone." She was proud of who she was, but also described the work it took to get there. In fact, she said "I spent most of my 20s and part of my 30s dismantling the person I had become based on other people's expectations of me."

As an adult, she dealt with serious anger problems. She described these problems as "reactive rage and the instinct to burn shit to the ground" every time she is triggered. Her anger came out under predictable circumstances: when she felt misunderstood or out of control. "That's a huge trigger," she said, "when my motives and my integrity is questioned." She said she tries to hold herself to a high moral standard regarding how she treats people. When she is questioned, she personalizes it.

She also described a lot of anger on the road. She drove a lot as part of her job, sometimes three or so hours per day. She said that the behavior of other drivers made her feel like she was taking her life into her hands every day at work. As she described it, driving provoked both a sense of helplessness and frustration regarding how other people behaved. This probably came back to the high moral standard she had for herself. She tried to be considerate and thoughtful and was angered by the thoughtlessness of others.

How she expressed this rage depended on the circumstances. In the car, she would scream, swear, or honk her horn. In other circumstances, such as in close relationships, she would shut down. She would retreat inward and even into a "spiral of self-loathing and depression." She said she hates conflict and tries to avoid it. She feels "out of control and helpless in that situation." That's why the car is the one place she expressed it outwardly.

The car feels to her like a safe place because no one can hear her and because they are strangers.

So where did all this come from for Simone? She told me that she's just recently started to realize some things about her childhood and the impact it had. "From the outside looking in, I had a pretty privileged childhood and adolescence and upbringing," she told me. "We lived in a house with a yard and drove big cars, and my father wore a suit and tie to work every day." Her basic needs were more than met. She was clothed and fed and sheltered. Her parents had high standards for achievement so she did well in school and they helped pay for her advanced education.

At the same time, though, Simone was suffering pretty severe emotional abuse and neglect. She was never allowed to express negative emotions. Her parents were alcoholics who hadn't intended to have her, and her father was the victim of horrendous child abuse when he was young. They got sober when she was five years old, but they were young when she was born and "didn't know what they were doing."

She said to me, "I wasn't allowed to have any of my feelings." She was a sensitive and smart kid who questioned everything, and she thinks this made her dad uncomfortable. He wanted to feel like he was succeeding as a parent and that meant having well-behaved children who were under his control. "As long as he could control his children and we showed the world how obedient, well-behaved, and quiet we were, he was succeeding and winning at life."

He controlled them through "terror and gaslighting." She wasn't allowed to have any of the normal emotions of a child. Any time she was upset about anything, she was punished. She was scolded for showing any form of negative emotion. "Stop crying or I'll give you something to cry about," he would say. At the same time, he had essentially weaponized the abuse he had experienced as a child to justify his emotional abuse and neglect of her, telling her she didn't have it nearly as bad as he did and so she shouldn't complain.

As an adult, Simone is doing the work of dealing with all this. She's in therapy, working through her discomfort with conflict and her anger problems. She said to me that, "in a perfect world, people have done the work to not be insensitive, invalidating, and dismissive." She wants to feel understood more than anything else. "So much of my childhood was feeling that nobody understood," she told me. What she really wants is for people to be honest with her and to listen to her.

The Emotions of Infants

Like Nathan in the previous chapter, in Simone you see a really powerful picture of how someone's emotions as adults are rooted in their childhood experiences and development. Simone wasn't allowed to show her negative* emotions as a kid. She was scolded or worse when she showed anger, fear, or sadness, and those reactions from her dad scared her. This is one of the ways we learn what emotions are ok to feel and express and what ones are not ok to feel and express.

Our understanding of how anger develops in human beings is rooted in how emotion, more generally, develops in human beings, and it starts in infancy. The emotions of infants are exceedingly simple. When they are first born, there is essentially contentment and displeasure (as displayed through crying). That displeasure typically arrives from not having physical needs met. Infants cry when they are hungry, tired, need to be changed, too hot or too cold, and so on. Those tears and wails are essentially a complaint about something negative going on in their life and a mechanism to get their needs met. Along with that, there's a startle response which is a very basic expression of fear, but really not much else in the way of emotional experiences and

---

* I really try not to categorize emotions as positive or negative. I don't see them that way. Our emotions are simply feeling states that give us information about the world, much like hunger, thirst, or other physiological states. That said, they can feel very negative to people, as they did to Simone.

expressions. Even intentional smiling, an early emotional expression, emerges a month or so after the baby is born.*

These basic emotional experiences and expressions turn into more advanced emotional experiences and expressions over time. As we mature physically and cognitively, we become capable of feeling new things and expressing them in new ways. Our physical development means we might encounter new provocations. Our improved vision means we can better see our caregivers' faces to exchange smiles with them. It also means, though, that we can see them leave the room, giving us something new to be sad about. Our ability to walk might give us a sense of excitement, but it also exposes us to new dangers to be frightened of, such as a flight of stairs or a hot stove. We use our newfound physical maturation to express our emotions differently too. Smiling, punching, running away, and voicing our emotions are all things we have to learn to do.

Our intellectual development is also responsible for these changes. When we are born, we have no idea that other people might be evaluating or judging us. As we mature, we start to realize that other human beings are independent and have different motivations than us. This recognition gives rise to new emotions like shame, embarrassment, and pride. In terms of anger, though, it gives rise to more subtle understandings of how and why provocations might happen. As an infant, you might get frustrated simply because you wanted something and didn't get it. As you mature, though, you develop an understanding of why you didn't get the thing you wanted. Maybe that helps alleviate the anger (they won't give it to me because it's dangerous) or maybe that makes the anger worse (they won't give it to me because they're mean).

---

* Parents often dispute this. "My baby started smiling right away" they tell me. The key word here is "intentional." Those early smiles are typically not intentional. It takes time for babies to learn to move their mouth muscles intentionally, and even more time to learn that this is a way they can express pleasure and happiness.

ANGER FACT

People sometimes inadvertently reinforce another's anger before the anger is even fully expressed. They are so worried about someone's tantrum, that they walk on eggshells to prevent the outburst.

Our individual differences in how we experience and express our anger develop in part through this emotional learning history. As we develop emotionally, we figure out how to feel about things through our exposure to our caregivers and how they feel about things. There are three basic psychological concepts here that explain most of this emotional development: reinforcement, punishment, and modeling.

Reinforcement, Punishment, and Modeling

Reinforcement and punishment are some of the most basic, yet misunderstood concepts in psychology. You can think of them this way. If you're trying to increase a behavior (for example, saying "please" and "thank you"), you're using reinforcement. If you're trying to decrease a behavior (hitting), you're using punishment. So if you praise a child for saying please, you're using positive reinforcement, but if you scold them for crying, like Simone's dad did to her, you're using punishment. These are instances where the rewards and punishments are intentional, and that happens a fair amount with emotion, but a lot of behavior reinforcement and punishment is unintended.

In fact, we see these unintentional reinforcements and punishments quite a bit with emotional development (this is sometimes what people mean when they talk about "natural consequences"). We have these innate expressions of emotion, some that are present at birth (such as crying, being startled) and some that emerge a little later on as we develop (smiling). These expressions are either reinforced or punished by our caregivers, sometimes intentionally and sometimes unintentionally. When a child cries, for example, a parent might say something like, "Hey now, big boys like you don't cry." Yet, a different parent may respond to that same behavior with, "That's ok. You can let it out." These two children learn very different messages about the appropriateness of tears. Child one was punished via a mild scolding for crying and child two was reinforced for it via gentle praise. The first child will likely try harder to hold their tears in next time. The second child will be more likely to let it out.

TIP

Think about the things you might do to reinforce another person's anger expressions. Do you give in to what they want immediately or try to resolve the situation for them to lessen the anger?

These reinforcements and punishments don't just happen through our caregivers, though. Children get them from their peers as well. When they show fear at school, they might be mocked by a classmate. When they are stoic, brave or maybe even aggressive, though, they might be praised for their "coolness" and "toughness." What might this look like with regard to anger? Well, let's imagine some of the ways we might reward or punish particular angry expressions during childhood.

Anger tends to be one of those emotions that caregivers send very clear messages about, likely because of its relationship to aggression and violence. When kids are angry, they often lash out physically or verbally in ways that might be dangerous or that caregivers don't want to encourage. Those lashing-out behaviors are usually dealt with quickly, so children are often immediately scolded for particular expressions. For instance:

- Getting punished for yelling at a sibling.
- Being made to go to their room until they cool off.
- Being reprimanded for swearing out of frustration.
- Being praised for taking deep breaths.
- Being taught and then praised for going and punching a pillow or a stuffed animal.*

But these are just examples of the overt and intentional rewards and punishments that come with anger (these are the ones that parents and teachers dole out on purpose). Because anger is a social emotion (we most frequently feel it in the context of social situations), there are all sorts of natural rewards and punishments that emerge. A parent might be so scared of a child's tantrums, for example, that they repeatedly give into the child's anger, rewarding and encouraging it for next time. The child then learns that their anger can be a tool for getting what they want. Alternatively, a child's angry outburst may alienate a friend or otherwise damage the relationship. They may learn from this that anger is scary and potentially harmful. Other examples include:

- Being praised by peers for standing up for yourself.
- Punching something and hurting your hand.
- Bullying a classmate and getting what you want from them.

---

* Unfortunately, this is a very common teaching from parents and psychologists. The idea being that we want to teach kids to let out their anger in a safe way so they don't bottle it up and hurt themselves. We have a lot of evidence, though, that this sort of catharsis only encourages anger and aggression.

In the 1950s, this perspective on learning, referred to as *behaviorism*, was the dominant view in psychology. Most behaviorists at the time, in fact, were not concerned about emotion at all. Since feelings like anger weren't observable behaviors, they focused on the actions and expressions associated with them. Instead of studying and talking about anger, they studied and talked about aggression. Instead of studying fear, they studied avoidance (the behavior most often associated with fear). This, though, had a really limiting impact on the field, especially when it comes to emotion.

In 1961, though, a study was done that really helped shift this way of thinking. Strict behaviorists would argue that behaviors are learned purely through rewards and punishments. We learn to be aggressive because we're rewarded for that aggression either intentionally or unintentionally. This 1961 research study – arguably one of the three most famous psychology studies of all time – found something quite unexpected (at least in terms of this narrow thinking in terms of rewards and punishments).

If you aren't familiar with Dr. Albert Bandura's "Bobo Doll Study"[28] it's either because you didn't take an introduction to psychology course or because you took an introduction to psychology course a long time ago and forgot about this particular project. It's very unlikely that the study wasn't covered. The idea behind the Bobo Doll Study was really simple – 72 children, ages three to six, were exposed to either an adult who was punching a bobo doll or interacting nicely with a bobo doll. For those of you unfamiliar with what a bobo doll is, it's essentially an inflatable punching bag with sand or something else heavy at the bottom so that it will bounce back up when hit, looking like a clown or something and as tall as the child. The participants, regardless of group, got to go into a room with the bobo doll to see how they interacted with it after witnessing the adult's interaction with one. In a result that will not surprise a single parent reading this, yet still revolutionized the way psychologists think about learning, the kids who watched the adult punch a bobo doll... punched the bobo doll. The kids who watched the adult interact nicely with the bobo doll interacted nicely with the bobo doll.*

In so many ways, this result feels obvious. But as I mentioned, in 1961 when this study was done, psychology was in a very different place. Learning was thought to happen largely through those reinforcements and punishments I described above. The idea that we learned behaviors by watching others, now referred to as modeling, was not accepted science yet. In fact, these findings were so monumental that Dr. Bandura was called to testify before the United States Congress several times in the late 1960s to discuss the potential effects of televised violence.

How does this play out with emotion more generally and anger more specifically? Well, we watch and learn from how our caregivers experience and express their emotions. If a child watches an adult yell and scream as a way of dealing with their anger, the child will likely yell and scream. If a child sees their parents cry when angry, they will likely start to cry when angry. In fact, a golden rule of emotional development is that kids tend to experience and express their emotions the way their caregivers do. Parents who express positive emotions in positive ways tend to have kids who express positive emotions in positive ways (and vice-versa).

Now remember Simone who learned via modeling of her father that anger was to be expressed outwardly by yelling, yet was also punished via scolding or worse when she expressed her anger that way. It helps explain why she so feels that desire to lash out but can only do so in the safety of her car or when she's alone. The messages she received were so mixed that they left her conflicted about the way to express herself.

Like I described with both Simone and my son, children essentially learn their expressions by watching their caregivers and other important people in their lives. Taking it a step

---

* Even though this is often referred to as a single study, it was actually an entire line of research related to social learning. It was replicated many times using several different variations, not just by Bandura but by many other scholars after him.

further, it's not just that they notice the anger of others and emulate it, it's that they intentionally look to others to see how they are responding to situations as a way of determining how they should feel. This is called social referencing and here's how it works. When we encounter a new stimulus and we aren't sure how to feel, we look to a trusted other, often a caregiver, to see how they feel. If they seem scared, we get scared. If they get angry, we get angry.* Over time, these collective experiences teach us what types of situations we should become angry over. The same way that we develop phobias in part by watching mom or dad express fear in response to particular objects or situations, we develop our anger responses by watching mom or dad get angry in particular situations. We start to prioritize particular types of injustice and unfairness because the people we look up to care about those injustices.

Display Rules

Interestingly, it is also here that children often learn their culture's display rules for particular emotions. Display rules are the informal norms that exist regarding how emotions should and should not be displayed in a particular culture or group. There's a well-established norm in most cultures, for example, that males should avoid crying. Despite popular claims, though, this difference isn't rooted so much in biology. It's rooted in cultural expectations. Male and female infants cry at the same rate[29], but males learn over time through rewards, punishments, and modeling that they should avoid crying.

Anger, in particular, has very complicated display rules. Who gets to be angry and in what way is driven largely by cultural and social expectations and they differ based on gender, race, age, and a variety of other factors. For instance, consider these three facts:

---

* This doesn't stop as we age. It happens less often because we are uncertain about our emotions less often, but it still happens. Have you ever been in a work meeting and had a colleague say something you were unsure about? Did you look to a trusted colleague or friend to see how they felt about it?

- Black men in the United States are more likely to be assigned anger management as a consequence for crimes, even when it's a similar type of crime or the same judge.[30]
- Women who express their anger outwardly are seen as less competent than men who express their anger in the exact same way.[31]
- Black men and women who voiced anger were found to be less influential than their white male counterparts when expressing the exact same thing.[32]

Taken together, it's clear that there are very different expectations for how people believe anger *should* be expressed based on gender and race. Anger can be expressed in the same way by two different people and how that expression is perceived will vary greatly depending on the characteristics of the angry person.

Let's consider what this means in the context of how anger develops in people. It really goes back to those three elements we discussed: reinforcement, punishment, and modeling. It provides very clear evidence that people are rewarded and punished differently for their anger. Women, for instance, are punished via negative appraisal when they express their anger outwardly. Men, though, are rewarded via positive appraisal for the same type of expression. What follows from this is that woman are likely to suppress their anger to avoid such negative appraisals while men will likely externalize their anger because they are so often rewarded for it.

This has indirect consequences on modeling as well. People are more likely to model the behavior of those who are similar to them, so boys tend to model the expressions of a male caregiver and girls tend to model the expressions of a female caregivers. The fact that men tend to externalize their anger by yelling or through physical aggression means that boys in their life will see that and be more likely to replicate it. It ends up a continuing cycle of gendered expression styles.

Emotional Development Doesn't Stop

As is obvious at this point, Simone had to navigate all sorts of different developmental challenges. She was subject to these differing display rules and expectations just like everyone, but also got mixed messages from her caregivers about appropriate expression styles. What I found fascinating about my conversation with her, though, was her continued dedication to relearn how to feel and express her feelings. She accurately described it as "work" and said she's spent the past decade or two *dismantling* the person she had become as a result of her childhood.

While not everyone does so with as much intention as Simone has, her continued work speaks to something really important about emotional development – it doesn't stop just because you're older. Our feelings continue to change as a result of our interactions, modeling, rewards, punishments, and so on. In adolescence, for instance, we not only mature physically in ways that influence anger – the maturational effects of testosterone and estrogen become more relevant here – we also mature socially in ways that influence our emotions.

A hallmark of adolescence is what we often refer to as emotional autonomy, and it is when kids start to disconnect emotionally from their parents and lean more on their peers to help meet their emotional needs. In adolescence, then, our parents become the source of our anger rather than the cure for it. Such emotional autonomy isn't just normal, it's healthy. Ultimately, an emotionally intelligent and healthy person is one who can manage their own emotions without assistance from caregivers or friends.

As we continue to age, we start to prioritize positive feeling states over negative ones. Referred to as *socioemotional selectivity*, we become less willing to tolerate negative emotions like fear, anger, and sadness later in life.[33] There becomes a growing sense that life is short and it's not worth spending too much time feeling bad. Adults, especially older adults, tend to avoid those negative feelings by sticking to activities where they feel comfortable. They tend to prefer the company of close friends over meeting new people, prioritize relationships over strenuous or challenging goals, and they tend to skip situations and people that make them angry. They might avoid reading about current events, for instance, or avoid relationships with people they find frustrating.

This tendency to avoid negative feelings isn't inherently good or bad for them. It really depends on the outcome and how it might be affecting them. For example, if their tendency to ignore current events leaves them unaware of important issues they should know, it might be a problem. If skipping emotionally strenuous activities means that they don't engage in some healthy activities they should be doing (learning new things, spending time with family), it might be something they should change. At the same time, though, if ignoring these emotionally draining people and situations simply means they enjoy their life more without consequence, that's perfectly fine.

Final Thought on Reinforcements and Punishments

We sometimes forget that rewards and punishments continue over the course of our lifespan. They aren't just a thing that happens when we are kids. Emotional patterns, therefore, can develop and change even in later life. Those patterns can also be specific to particular relationships in that how you emote with your parents might be different from how you emote with your spouse or your children. It is likely that those patterns are associated with how rewarding or punishing you feel those interactions are. If you have a friend who makes you feel safe enough to express your anger and it is therefore rewarding, you'll likely express it. If you have a colleague, though, who inadvertently shames you for venting at work, you'll likely stop or find a new person to vent to.

For example, thinking back to the case study from chapter 1, when Izzy spoke of how her dad's anger was often directed at the people he knew well rather than at his co-workers or strangers

– though I don't know for sure, I imagine this is because he was rewarded for that anger in ways he wouldn't be if he expressed it that way at work. If he were to speak to or yell at a co-worker or boss the way he spoke to or yelled at Izzy, there would be consequences. Similarly, he might have actually felt rewarded for expressing his anger at Izzy in ways that went unrealized. Even though it was hurtful to Izzy, and likely led to guilt for him eventually, in the moment it must have felt good to him, which served as a reinforcement. These rewards and punishments might be subtle and hard to recognize without stepping back from it.

ACTIVITY: WHERE DID THEY LEARN THAT?

Returning to that angry person in your life, answer the following about them (to the degree that you can):

1. What aspects of their learning history (for example, rewards, punishments, modeling) might have led to their anger?
2. How has their anger changed as they've aged?
3. Is their anger expression style consistent across relationships or do they express it differently with some people?
4. What are some ways that their anger expression style might be reinforced in their relationship with you? What are some ways other expressions might be punished in their relationship with you?

The Contagiousness of Rage

Simone's anger was informed both directly and indirectly by her relationship with her parents, especially her father. And as you can see, this is often the case. Angry people are created from a foundation of DNA and learning history. They might be born from predispositions to be angry, along with an upbringing that brings out that rage. At the same time, though, we are influenced by the moment and the people around us. Emotions can be contagious and angry people can emerge, not because of a complicated life story or because they were predisposed to be that way, but simply because the people around them bring it out of them. In the next chapter, we'll talk about how anger can be influenced by the world around us in a given situation.

CHAPTER 4

THE CONTAGIOUSNESS OF ANGER

"I Absolutely Snapped"

In May of 2010, a group came together in Columbus, Ohio to protest the Affordable Care Act (ACA), President Obama's signature healthcare initiative (often referred to as Obamacare). The protest itself was one of many happening across the United States and wouldn't necessarily have been noteworthy on its own had it not been for a viral video that captured a particular person behaving very badly. Like a lot of these protests, a group of counter-protesters arrived as well and this particular counter-protest included a man named Robert Letcher who was holding a sign that read "Got Parkinson's? I do and you might. Thanks for your help."

Letcher is sitting down in front of the anti-ACA protesters when a man leans down and lectures him, condescendingly, "If you're looking for a handout, you're in the wrong end of town. There's nothing for free over here. You have to work for everything you get." Meanwhile, another man comes over and says, "No, no, I'll pay for this guy. Here you go." He tries to hand Letcher money, which Letcher doesn't take, so he drops the bill on him. "Start a pot," he says, "I'll pay for you." He then starts to walk away, but turns back and yells, "I'll decide when to give you money." He then crumples up another bill and throws it at Letcher, yelling even louder, "No more handout!" The crowd behind them seems to be egging him on, applauding his hostility and calling Letcher a communist.

Taken together, what you have is a particularly troubling sight where a large group of people, led by two men, are mocking an elderly Parkinson's patient. The video went viral almost immediately and it wasn't long before one of the men was identified. Chris Reichert denied it was him at first but about a week later acknowledged that he was the person who threw money at Letcher.

To be honest, I'm less interested in the contents of the video than I am in what Reichert had to say about it a few weeks later. Frankly, there are a lot of videos online of belligerent, hostile, and angry people treating other people poorly. Usually the angry person isn't identified, though, so you know very little information about what happened, how they typically behave, or their values. In this case, though, Reichert spoke up about what he did and why he did it.

"I snapped. I absolutely snapped and I can't explain it any other way. He's got every right to do what he did and some may say I did, too, but what I did was shameful. I haven't slept since that day." He went on to say, "That was my first time at any political rally and I'm never going to another one."

We could have a lengthy conversation about whether this apology was genuine or if this was just an attempt to minimize the damage to his image. There was a great deal of anger directed toward him and he voiced some concerns about his safety when later interviewed. My best guess is that this apology is a little bit genuine and a little bit damage control. What I find particularly interesting, though, is his acknowledgement that being at this political rally brought the anger out of him. His response, whether he meant the apology or not, acknowledges a simple truth about our anger: it can be contagious.

Case Study: Sarah – "This anger felt unhinged"

Sarah works as the artistic director for a 2,000-seat performing arts center. Like just about every other performing arts center in the United States, they closed their doors in March 2020 because of the Covid-19 health crisis. It was an emotionally painful experience for her and her staff. As Sarah described it to me, they do the work they do because they want to bring joy to their patrons. She and her team take their work seriously, not just because they love the arts, but because they know the value of the arts to the community. Sarah said to me:

"Our goal is always to make the patron experience as enjoyable as possible. Because we know that the act of connecting with a live performer on stage has a genuine positive impact on their wellbeing and then what happens simultaneous to that is their connection to the rest of the audience. I often quote a study that audience members' heartbeats will sync up during a performance. There's a real thing that happens here and to us on our end of it, because we've chosen to work in this industry, that is a real very special thing to us. We want to do everything we can to make sure that that happens every single time for everyone that comes here. That they feel what that feels like."

You can imagine how devastating it must have been for Sarah to have to end live performances the way she did. Once it became clear how long the shut-down was going to last, Sarah told her staff: "Just think of the joy and celebration we're going to experience when we come out of this. When we're finally able to reconvene patrons in our building, it is going to be for the purpose of joy and celebration, and just think how desperately our community will need that."

They reopened for their first performance in September 2021, a full 18 months later, but it did not end up feeling joyful or celebratory. This particular center, like many others, was requiring masks to prevent the spread of Covid-19. Sarah said she went into this performance expecting some anger from the patrons. By now, she had heard from other centers that people in certain communities were not responding well to the mask requirements so they had prepared the staff for potential disputes. She had instructed them to be relatively nonconfrontational, to offer a friendly reminder and a mask when necessary, and not to go back to the same person twice. If someone refused to comply, they should elevate it to a floor manager or to Sarah. Again, the goal was to try and provide a positive, friendly, and enjoyable experience for everyone.

This first performance was a family program with a target age of young children, ages two to five. "It was clear right out of the gate, that it wasn't just going to be just one angry patron," she said. "I've had patrons who didn't like something and wanted a refund. Or didn't like the way their interaction with an usher went. But… this anger felt unhinged. You would see a mom standing there with a three-year-old, and the mom's face would be inches from the face of a volunteer, a 75-year-old volunteer, and the mom would be screaming at the top of her lungs. Calling her a baby-killer, because she had offered a mask to the child."

At the same time, though, Sarah expressed a lot of empathy for some patrons. "Now, I also saw moms, sitting just in total misery trying to get their kids to wear a mask. So, how we were all feeling was really complicated because I did have great compassion for those parents. I have really vivid memories of moms sitting on benches in tears themselves. Their kids weren't expected to wear masks anywhere else in our community. Parents had invested in trying to create this special day after what had been a really hard year and a half for everyone."

Sarah had decided to position herself outside the center as people arrived in order to provide a cushion before people got to the front doors. She said things got a little congested at the doors as people showed their tickets so she thought she would offer a friendly heads up about the need to wear masks outside the building before people got to the ticket-takers. Patrons had also received this information when purchasing their tickets and another reminder before they attended the show, so it should not have been a surprise. "Part of what I was trying to do was absorb the blows before they got to the staff." One of the more memorable interactions she had from this spot was when she offered an unmasked family a friendly reminder that there were masks available inside the doors if they needed them. "The woman turned to her husband and said 'I told you.'" He responded to this by shouting, not necessarily at Sarah, "But for the benefit of everyone around, fuck this!"

Sarah followed this family as they moved toward the doors because the anger was "so demonstrative. It was really loud and it was for the benefit of other people." This was true of several instances she dealt with that day. "It felt performative. I'm not saying that it wasn't genuine or that they weren't feeling some sort of rage, but there was also a real effort to make sure everybody around them was seeing it and hearing it. That felt dangerous also. I could tell there was something going on where people were posturing and hoping to engage more people into their rage."

She saw a volunteer going to approach him and she intercepted, asking him to go outside to talk more about this, "mainly because there were so many children in the area." She said part of her hoped he would just end up leaving, and that maybe his wife would stay and take the kids to see the show without him. "He ended up putting a mask on but first he called me a fucking cunt. I don't know that I've ever been called that to my face before. I was called a fucking bitch a lot that day, at least eight to ten times. I was only called a cunt twice."

This particular person was not the most troubling person Sarah dealt with that day. There was another man whose behavior looked so dangerous to her that they ended up getting the police involved. "He made a big show of taking his mask off, and was flipping off employees." Multiple people came to Sarah and said they were concerned about him. When the police arrived and asked Sarah what she thought they should do, Sarah said, "I'm not going to ask you to physically remove this person from a theater full of children, including his own." The show was almost over so they were going to let things go and just get through it.

The problem, though, was that there was a special event after the show where some attendees could meet and talk with the performers. It was clear that this particular person was planning on attending this event too, so he wasn't leaving. Sarah asked the police to ask him to wait outside. He was escorted outside but then ended up waiting by the windows and looking through at Sarah and the other staff. She likened him to caged animal, stalking back and forth across the window like a tiger at a zoo. She started to question whether or not she would be safe to leave the building later that day or if she needed the police to walk her to her car.

In the end, she said she got through it. She and her staff had a lot of conversations about what they should do different next time, or even if they should keep trying. She cried a lot too. She said she kept coming back to the fact that "they didn't have to be there. We were offering full refunds." If people weren't willing to put on a mask, they could have left without consequence. But she also told me, demonstrating a really impressive ability to empathize and understand the situation from their perspective, "I don't think their expectations were actually that unreasonable." Such mask policies, even when in place, weren't being enforced elsewhere in her community. "Many places they went required masks but then didn't actually enforce that requirement." Her patrons probably knew they were supposed to wear masks, but just assumed, like so many other places, it wouldn't be enforced.

Emotional Contagion

Sarah's story is intriguing from a number of perspectives, and we'll revisit it often throughout the book. But what I find most fascinating in the context of this chapter, is her description of how people were actively *trying* to rile each other up. Covid wasn't the only thing that was contagious that day. Their anger was too, and while they were ambivalent about spreading the virus, they were actively trying to spread the rage.

Over a decade ago, some students and I worked on a project related to this very topic.[34] We provided participants with some vignettes, brief case studies, describing an emotional situation. The participants were to imagine they were going out to eat for a special occasion. They had booked reservations way in advance, but when they got to the restaurant, there was a long line and obvious problems with the reservation system. When the person right in front of them spoke to the host, that person was told their reservation had been lost. The person reacted with one of two emotions (depending on the version of the story), anger or sadness, either crying or yelling about how the restaurant had ruined their evening. That person than left the restaurant either visibly angry or visibly sad. The vignette ended with the participant then going to the host and being told that their reservation had also been lost.

We then asked participants to indicate how angry, sad, scared, or happy they would feel if this happened to them. Obviously, no one indicated that they would feel happy and very few indicated that they would feel scared. How angry or sad they became, though, depended in part on whether or not the person in front of them in line was angry or sad. The participants who had an angry person in line in front of them got angrier. The participants who had a sad person ahead of them got sadder. They essentially used the emotion of the person in front of them as an indicator of how they should feel in that moment. You can think of this as a variation of that social referencing I described in the previous chapter. We look to those around us, knowingly or unknowingly, to see how we should feel in a given moment.

ANGER FACT

Injustice is a greater source of anger than having your goals blocked, according to survey responses gathered by The Anger Project.[35]

There's a good reason we do this and it's rooted in our evolutionary history. When we are in a group of people, it's advantageous for us to feel what they are feeling and to act accordingly. Our ancestors, human and nonhuman, for instance, would have benefited from this sort emotional contagion. If the people around me are scared, there might be a real threat to our safety, so I should be scared too. If the people around me are angry, we might have been wronged or treated unfairly, so I should be angry too. Since our emotions are motivators that encourage us to protect ourselves by fleeing or fighting back, those emotional cues I get from the people around might be lifesaving.

Emotional contagion is a well-studied phenomenon with research linking it to everything from empathy enhancement to workplace burnout. It is relevant to one-on-one interactions, small group dynamics at work, friends, families, and larger scale events like protests, mobs, and riots. At its most basic, we find that seeing a person smile motivates us to smile and seeing them frown motivates us to frown. In 1998, Drs. Ulf Dimberg and Monika Thunberg[36] did three studies where they showed participants pictures of happy or angry faces and measured their reactions by measuring muscle activation of the face. They attached electrodes to particular muscle groups and they found that seeing a pictures of happy or angry faces led to activation in facial muscles consistent with the photos. Happy faces led to smiling. Angry faces led to frowning.

Epinephrine, Euphoria, and Anger

Two researchers, Drs. Stanley Schachter and Jerome Singer, did a fascinating study[37] on this back in 1962. Using a fair amount of deception, they recruited participants to take part in a study they told them was about how vitamins would influence their vision. As such, they gave them all shots. Half received epinephrine (adrenaline) and the other half got a placebo (regardless, they were all told the shots were vitamin supplements). The dosage of epinephrine they used would provide, as they described it in the article, "almost a perfect mimicry of a discharge of the sympathetic nervous system" (for example, slight heart rate, blood pressure, and breathing increases that started about 5 minutes after the shot and lasted around 20 minutes).

Participants were given one of three sets of information about the shot: epinephrine informed (told what will happen as a result of the shot), epinephrine ignorant (told nothing), and epinephrine misinformed (given incorrect information about the effects of the shot). After this, a "stooge" entered the room. This was actually a member of the research team but was acting as another participant. The participant and the stooge were then given instructions to wait for 20 minutes before they took the eye test. During that time, the stooge behaved in one of two ways, providing yet another variable to the study: angry or euphoric.*

In the euphoric condition, the stooge was playful and fun. He doodled on some scratch paper, played a game of garbage-can basketball with crumpled-up paper, and encouraged the other player to get involved too. He made paper airplanes, played with a hula hoop, and said things like, "I feel like a kid again."† In the anger condition, the stooge and the participant are given surveys to complete. The stooge behaves grumpily in this condition, complaining about the length of the survey and getting angry about some of the questions. The survey itself is intended to be angering, with questions such as "With how many men (other than your father) has your mother had extramarital relationships?"

So if you're playing along at home, we have three different independent variables here, epinephrine or placebo (two levels), information about the shot (three levels), angry or euphoric (two levels), for eighteen different research categories. What the researchers were really interested in here was not vision as the participants were told, but rather, the happiness or anger the participants experienced going through the study. These were

---

* I do think this study is fascinating and it's informed a lot of my work. That said, I probably wouldn't have called the positive condition "euphoric." Maybe… "mildly upbeat?"

† Sounds just like euphoria, doesn't it?

measured through observations of the participant's behavior and a survey at the end of the study.

Imagining you're a participant in this study, you've got a couple of different sources of information. Are you having a physiological reaction to the epinephrine? Were you accurately informed what that reaction would feel like? Is the person in the room with you angry or happy? Most interesting to me is the group who received a shot and didn't know what it would do. This is the group that I would expect to be most likely to take on the emotions of the stooge. They are having a mild, emotion-like physiological response, and were not expecting it. To explain that reaction, they might look to their environment.

Indeed, that's what happened. Participants who had been uninformed or even misinformed about how their body would react to the shot were more likely to become happy when the stooge was happy and angry when the stooge was angry. In the euphoric condition, they joined in on the fun and even engaged in some entertaining activities the stooge wasn't engaging in. Plus, they just said they were happier on a self-report scale. For anger, similar findings. If they did not know what the impact of the shot would be, they got angry along with the stooge.

I like to think about this study in terms of Sarah's story above. While no one at the show was given shots of epinephrine that day, there was undoubtedly some elevated tension and anxiety associated with being in public and in a crowded space. Many of those patrons probably were having a physiological reaction consistent with an epinephrine burst simply because they were nervous about being out. Did they recognize that or did they attribute it to the frustration of what they considered unreasonable masking policies? Did they pick up on the anger of their fellow theater-goers* in the same way participants picked up on the anger of the stooges?

---

* The "performative" nature of their anger as Sarah described it sure makes it seem like they are *intentionally* playing the stooge here.

One final interesting but unexpected finding from this study is that some participants who had not been informed or had been misinformed of the shot's effects still attributed their physiological state to the shot. They indicated so much in the survey, saying that they assumed the heart-rate increase was the result of the shot. The researchers went back and coded that group as "self-informed" to separate their data from the rest and see the impact of that attribution. When they did, they found that this group got less angry and less happy than the other participants, essentially adding one more piece of data to support the idea that we look to our surroundings for emotional cues.

Our Environment Matters

There's a lot to unpack here regarding what all this means for the angry people in your life. Know that people are influenced by the moods of those around them, including yours. It is one element of any situation that informs their thinking, feelings, and behaviors. Your spouse, your co-workers, your friends, your kids – they all unknowingly base their feelings on the emotions of others, and what you are feeling in a given moment when you're around them becomes part of their emotional experience.

The emotions of others aren't the only factors they might unknowingly base their emotions on. There's a variety of research that points to some often unrecognized influencers. For instance:

1. The color red was shown to increase the likelihood people perceived facial expressions to be angry.[38]
2. People were more likely to be aggressive online when they believed they were anonymous.[39]
3. Uncomfortable outdoor temperatures are associated with increased online hate speech.[40]

The idea here is not that we need to try and understand each and every environmental factor that might cause anger. That would be impossible. The point is that we should understand that there are environmental factors in any situation (such as how loud it is, time of day) that might be contributing to the person's anger.

The other thing to note about emotional contagion is that angry people influence the moods of those around them. The hostility Sarah witnessed and experienced at the theater that day was a troubling example of not just how anger can spread, but how it can be spread intentionally. What I found most haunting in my conversation with her was how she described the anger as seeming "performative." There was this intentional effort from some of the angry patrons to rile the other visitors up into a bit of an angry frenzy. They wanted the other visitors to be angry too in the hopes that it would help them get their way. Emotional contagion was being used as a tool.

"Not a Prosocial Group"

After talking with Sarah, I started thinking about whether or not she was dealing with angry people that day… or whether she was dealing with an angry mob. The line isn't always clear. In fact, about four years ago, I spoke with Dr. Lori Rosenthal, a social psychologist who wrote a chapter on mob violence for the book *The Psychology of Good and Evil*,[41] about this very question. I was trying to figure out when a group of people goes from being a crowd to a mob. The answer isn't just that they are angry. You get angry crowds at sporting events. You get them at peaceful protests.*

Dr. Rosenthal helped answer this for me. She said: "A mob is a very specific type of crowd. It's an expressive crowd. The common purpose that they get together around is expressing emotion. Crowds can express emotions in positive ways, but mobs are expressing emotions in negative ways and there's a connotation of violence… either an intent to commit violence, a likelihood to commit violence, or they are actually committing violence. It's not a prosocial group."†

Sarah's patrons didn't get together that day to express anger and violence. They were there to see a show. But the way they were treating people, the way they were egging each other on, and the fact that violence felt like a real possibility to Sarah and her staff might make that first part moot. Who cares why they were there? What matters is how they felt and acted once they were there.

Dr. Rosenthal said something else really interesting that I think is relevant here too. She said: "Generally, in terms of historical research on social behavior, we have defined a crowd as being in physical proximity, but I think in today's society with our social-media connections, a crowd can actually exist in the virtual world." I would argue that if a crowd can exist online, a mob can too.

Take for example the story of Justine Sacco who in 2013 tweeted out an offensive attempt at a joke about AIDS right before boarding a plane to South Africa. She had fewer than 200 Twitter followers at the time, but in the 11 hours she was on the

---

* Remember that anger is just the feeling and not the action. Someone can be angry at a protest without being aggressive or violent. In fact, if they are at a protest, they are probably angry about something.

† We could really go down a rabbit hole here depending on how we define violence. Those anti-ACA protesters at the event that Reichert was at were attempting to prevent meaningful healthcare reform in the United States. Millions of Americans die every year from inadequate health coverage, so though they likely didn't think about it this way, they were advocating for the deaths of millions. Is that violence?

plane, her tweet was noticed and shared by media outlets and she became the center of a massive Twitterstorm. Since she was on a flight, she was disconnected from Twitter and was unaware of what was happening. She couldn't apologize or remove the tweet. In that time, an online mob had formed around her offensive and racist tweet. People were hurling cruel insults at her (including a number of slurs), some were calling for her to be fired (which she was), and some writing that they hoped she would get AIDS. One user even acknowledged that a mob had formed and tweeted out a picture of a mob of Simpsons' characters holding torches.

When she landed, she deleted the tweet, along with her Twitter, Facebook, and Instagram accounts. She issued an apology a day later.[42] The entire story is beautifully described in Jon Ronson's TED talk, "When online shaming goes too far."[43]

When a group of people come together online with the intent of expressing anger and/or harming people, it's an online mob. Anger is not just a common emotion online; some research has found it to be the most viral emotion online, with people more likely to share angering posts than sad, scary, disgusting, or happy ones.[44] The contagious effects of anger are felt in all walks of life.

Finally, it's worth noting that there was a very sweet and joyful example of emotional contagion hidden in Sarah's story about reopening. The research she shared with me on the syncing of heartbeats[45] is ultimately an example of how the power of emotional contagion can be used for good. When people come together for a common purpose, and that purpose includes sharing a positive emotional experience together, it can be profoundly moving. It may even help us overcome very real barriers that exist between us.

ACTIVITY: EXTERNAL CONTRIBUTORS

With that angry person in your life, think about a particular time they were really angry (whether it was with you or with someone else when you were around them).

1. In what way might the attitudes and emotions of the people around them have contributed to their anger in that moment?
2. What other aspects of the environment might have contributed to their anger in that moment?
3. Did those environmental factors influence the way the person interpreted the provocation that led to their anger?

Habitual and Consistent Negativity

Though the Schachter and Singer study says a lot about emotional contagion, it says just as much about the role of interpretation. When people didn't know the source of their physiological arousal, they looked for an interpretation that made sense to them. They used whatever information they had, accurate or inaccurate, to *decide* how to feel. Their feelings were influenced, not just by the people and the situation, but by their interpretation of the people and the situation.

As I've been discussing the factors that contribute to the experiences and expressions of angry people, I've not yet gotten to what I believe is the most important part: the worldview of the angry person. Because despite these genetic, neurological, developmental, and environmental contributions, the best predictor of whether or not someone is angry is their outlook. How they see the world, how they view other people, and how they interpret the circumstances right in front of them matter most. One of the things we know is that some people will habitually and consistently look at those circumstances in a way that makes them angry.

CHAPTER 5
THE WORLDVIEWS OF ANGRY PEOPLE

Reasoning on the Basis of False Assumptions

You can learn a lot about a person's belief system simply by listening to the statements they make when they are angry, sad, or scared. Moments of distress often bring out these quick, automatic statements that might reveal how they see themselves, how they see others, and how they perceive their own ability to cope. For instance, an angry person might use phrases like:

* People should just…
* They did that because…
* This happens every time…
* Well, now everything is ruined…

Phrases like this are what Dr. Aaron Beck, a brilliant and prolific psychiatrist, author, and scholar, described as automatic thoughts, and he believed that they offered an important window into how people view themselves and others. He also saw these thoughts as evidence of what causes most psychological distress. In fact, in 1986 he said: "Most psychological problems center on incorrectly appraising life's stresses, reasoning on the basis of false assumptions and jumping to self-defeating conclusions."[46]

It's difficult to truly put into words how influential Dr. Beck was in the fields of psychology and psychiatry. It wasn't just that he was prolific, having published more than 20 books, countless journal articles and book chapters, as well as quite a few psychological tests. It was that he paved the way for a new approach to understanding mental health. To quote an article in *The New York Times* written after his passing in 2021 concerning his methodology: "It was an answer to

Freudian analysis: a pragmatic, thought-monitoring approach to treating anxiety, depression and other mental disorders, and it changed psychiatry."

What is particularly fascinating about Beck's approach, though, is how he developed it in the first place. He was actually trained in psychodynamic theory and was a practicing psychoanalyst, meaning he used therapy techniques rooted in Freudian thinking. That might include things like dream interpretation, free association, or other strategies designed to get at a client's unconscious desires, thoughts, and memories. Over the years of practicing, though, he became less comfortable with this approach to therapy, believing it lacked scientific rigor and support.

His new approach to treatment evolved from his psycho-dynamic work with depressed clients. He often found such clients would make these disparaging comments about themselves. They would say things like, "I'm useless," "People don't like me," or "There's no hope." He later labeled these "automatic thoughts" and described them as the thoughts people have, often outside of awareness, that influence their feelings and behaviors. Though much of his work, especially his early work, was focused on depressed clients, he later began focusing on other forms of emotional distress, and even wrote a book about anger, hostility, and violence in 1999.[47] In it, he described the common thought types of angry people, which for him included egocentrism, tendencies to overgeneralize, and strong beliefs about how things should be. His thinking on this was heavily influential to the field and will serve as examples of a lot of the thought types I'll describe later in the chapter.

Case Study: Ephraim –
"When I perceive someone as thinking they know more than me"

Ephraim is a 30-year-old librarian in New York City. He is a self-described "angry person" who snaps easily. He said of his anger that it "comes on hot, sometimes out of nowhere, and burns itself out very quickly." He said he loves working in a library even though he isn't always what you would call a "people-person," and he is easily frustrated by the patrons. He's engaged and his fiancée, who he lives with, sees his anger the most. It's something they talk about quite a bit. He's been working on this with his therapist, and said he talks not just about his anger but also "the feelings I have about my anger."

"I've been angry ever since I was a kid. I didn't realize it too much until I was grown up and I was like… oh, I was awful. I was very angry and very awful because of it." When he snaps, as he describes it, he raises his voice, sometimes yelling at people around him. He said it's a very physical feeling for him. He feels it in his whole body. He described it as "a pressurized feeling and snapping is the physical way to release that tension." He said he never plans on it, so it isn't an intentional way he releases the tension. It just happens. In his relationship with his fiancée, he said he notices his anger because it scares her in the moment. She'll cower from him, so he knows it must be intimidating in ways he doesn't fully realize.

The situations in which he snaps say a lot about thoughts that are driving his anger. He was able to identify two overlapping types of situations that tend to bring out his anger: (1) when he feels misunderstood and (2) when he's interrupted. The second one is a little easier to break down. He told me he has attention deficit hyperactivity disorder (ADHD) so when he's trying to focus and people interfere, it can be frustrating. This happens a fair amount at work, and he acknowledged that it's sort of funny because his job is to help people. Yet when they come and ask him for help, he gets irritated because he's trying to work on some other project and it feels like they are slowing him down.

Feeling misunderstood, though, is a much more complicated psychological experience in a lot of ways. "It's when I perceive someone as thinking they know more than me. That makes me snap very quickly," he explained. "Whether or not they actually feel that way – if I think they are thinking, I could do this better than he is, it makes me very angry." Similarly, he told me,

"When I feel like someone's not understanding what I'm saying, it's another trigger for me." He said this happens a lot with his fiancée but also at work.

At the core of these angry outbursts is a feeling of not being valued. When he is interrupted, he perceives it as someone not valuing his time, his goals, or what he's working on. When people disagree with him, or he even thinks they might be disagreeing with him, he perceives it as someone not valuing his intellect or his abilities. I asked him if he knew the origin of that excessive need to feel valued. He laughed and said: "Big shock, I have a very controlling mother, who controlled everything I did... and said and wore and felt as a child. I was never allowed to do my own thing or feel my own feelings." He said he grew up feeling like nothing of his – his opinions, his time, his wants – was valued. He said a lot of his anger was directed at his mom when he was a kid. "We would get in screaming matches," he told me. He realizes now that they are both anxious people and that made things worse.

Ephraim has been in therapy working on this, and he's got some strategies for how to deal with his anger. The main thing for him has been healthy communication. When he's feeling angry, he tries to communicate that he needs some time to think through what he wants to say and to put his words together. He said that if he knows there's going to be a hard conversation, he'll sometimes start it through a text message so there's time for him to compose his thoughts and process the exchange. He said this has really improved his relationship with his mom.

This is related to what he wants from the people he's interacting with. "To give me time," he said. "If there's an elevated moment going on, and I don't respond right away, to not push it." He said that people sometimes think he's ignoring them when he takes that time, but that's not what's happening. He's just trying to put his feelings and words together. He actually said this is something he and his boss have worked on, coming up with strategies for how he can take that time even when he's working with patrons, by responding to their requests with, "Sure thing.

I'll be right over," so that it sounds friendly, lets them know he'll be there soon, and gives him the time he needs to feel collected and get to a good stopping point with what he's doing.

The Worldviews That Drive Our Anger

Ephraim provides a really interesting example of how an underlying worldview can drive particular automatic thoughts that lead to anger. At his core, he seems to have a fundamental belief that *the world does not understand him*. He goes into situations with this underlying value and it influences how he interprets his moment-to-moment interactions. This belief is a lens through which his experiences are filtered. Truthfully, Ephraim may be right that many people in the world don't understand him. There's no implication here that his or anyone's worldviews are incorrect or flawed. They simply exist as filters that influence how we experience the things we go through.

Beck defined these broader worldviews as schemas and he described what he called the "cognitive triad" which includes schemas about yourself, schemas about others, and schemas about the future. These are what Beck considered the three critical elements of a person's belief system. For instance, a depressed person might have an outlook like so:

- Self: I am inadequate. I am unsuccessful. I am worthless.
- The world/environment: People don't like me. People are better than me. People don't think I'm important.
- Future: The future is hopeless. Things will always be like this. Things will likely get worse.

Meanwhile, an angry person may have a cognitive triad that looks more like this:

- Self: I am entitled to certain things. My wants are more important than those of other people.

- The world/environment: People will let me down. People get in my way. The world is unfair/unjust.
- Future: The future is hopeless. People will continue to mess things up.

What this means is that these two people, the depressed and the angry, could experience the exact same situation, but see it through entirely different lenses and have entirely different emotional reactions.

TIP

Finding the nuance in situations or motivations of others so as not to think of them as all bad can help people lessen their anger.

Imagine, for instance that these two people are students who fail a test. The person with a depressed worldview might look at that experience and think, "Of course I failed it. I'm not smart enough and the teacher knows it. I'll probably fail the entire class now." The angry person, though, might externalize the cause and think, "This teacher doesn't know anything. I failed because the test was unfair and they didn't teach me well enough." Interestingly, they may come to the same conclusion, that they will fail the class, but for very different reasons. The first will fail because they think they don't have what it takes to be successful. The second will fail because they think the instructor isn't a good enough teacher.

Three Broad, Overlapping Categories of Thoughts

When it comes to the automatic thoughts of angry people, there are three broad, overlapping categories that tend to cause or at least exacerbate their anger: high expectations of others, dichotomous thinking, and disaster thinking.

High Expectations of Others

I recently described the following scenarios on social media and asked people how they would respond if it happened to them:

> You're driving along, going over the speed limit in the left lane, passing cars, going to get over as soon as you have a chance. The car behind you obviously wants to go faster, riding on your bumper. When you do have a chance to get over, they pass you on the right and then intentionally cut you off as a way of getting back at you for going slower than they wanted.

I then asked them what they might do in that situation. The idea was to get a sense for how people perceive the importance of revenge. Would they do nothing, honk, somehow go after the person, and so on. More than 2,000 people responded, many of them just answering the question I had posed. But many people responded, not with an answer to the question I asked, but with a repudiation of the scenario, telling me they would never be in this situation because they wouldn't drive as poorly as the person in my example. Specifically, they said they would have driven faster, gotten over quicker when they had the chance, or signaled earlier so the person wouldn't pass them on the right.

For the record, I think the protagonist in my example was driving responsibly and safely, but that isn't really the point here. What was interesting was how quickly so many people gravitated toward blaming not the obvious offender in the example, but the victim of that offense. They weren't mad at the person who intentionally cut someone off. Rather they were mad at the person they thought was driving too slow and not getting over quickly enough. Most of them stopped short of implying the person deserved to be cut off, but plenty of people implied that the initial driver was the one in the wrong.*

To me, this is a really interesting example of the way in which expectations of others and unwritten rules for behavior can play such a significant role in one's anger. People had their own ideas about how drivers should drive. Those ideas were not consistent with most laws (the offender in this scenario broke far more laws than the protagonist). Rather, their expectations were based on their own sense of what is right and wrong for how people should drive. They had these informal and clearly not universal norms for how to behave on the road, and they were mad not at the person who broke multiple actual laws, but at the person who violated their unwritten rules.†

This is one of the hallmarks of an angry personality. They often have some relatively strict rules for how people *should* behave, feel, and think, and when people violate those rules, they get angry. This may include some demandingness, blaming, mindreading, or even personalizing the behaviors of others. They put their own needs ahead of the needs of others, assume the worst of people and their motivations, and might even assign blame where it doesn't belong.

For Ephraim, this all-or-nothing thinking could be seen in how he jumped to conclusions regarding people's thoughts about him. He made assumptions about how people viewed him and those assumptions influenced his emotions. If he thought they thought he was stupid or that they could do things better than him, he got angry. He admitted that he had no reason to

---

* I know some people are just screaming at the book right now because of how wrong they think I am about this scenario. If you're one of those people, just hang on. We're going to get through this.

† I should note by the way that as soon as some people came out to defend the offender in this scenario, others came to defend the protagonist. Online arguments broke out over which not-real person in my not-real scenario was at fault. Such is social media.

assume they thought those things about him, but he jumped to that conclusion without evidence and got angry as a result.

Cognitive therapists have identified a number of these types of thoughts, not just related to anger, but associated more generally with emotional problems. Here is a shortlist of some of these thoughts with examples of how they connect to anger (note, though, that these thought types overlap considerably with one another).

- **Misattributing causation or blaming:** This is when people misinterpret what caused a situation or assign blame incorrectly. They might make assumptions about *why* a person did something or simply blame the wrong person. In the case of anger, this can be heard in statements like, "I bet he did that because…" or "They did that on purpose."
- **Demandingness:** This is when people put their own wants and desires ahead of the wants and desires of other people. They decide their needs are more important than the needs of others. When a waiter is slower than they would like, they might respond with "I don't care what he is doing, he needs to get over here."
- **Other-directed shoulds:** A variation on demandingness, other-directed shoulds are when people have strict beliefs about the ways that people *should* act. These rules may be consistent or inconsistent with the rules other people have (such as people should say please and thank you, people should never be late to a meeting). When people violate those rules, people get especially angry.* The driving situation above was a good example of these sorts of other-directed shoulds.

---

* Less relevant to this book, there is such a thing as self-directed shoulds that include rules about our own behavior (I should exercise every day, I should get all of this work done). People who engage in self-directed shoulds are more likely to get sad and feel angry at themselves. In fact, data from The Anger Project (www.alltheragescience.com) shows that 41 per cent of people are extremely likely to get angry with themselves.

- **Expectations of changed behaviors:** This occurs when people expect others will change in order to meet their expectations. They think their co-workers, friends, and family will change their behavior just for them. When people don't change for them in the way they expect, they get angry.

- **Jumping to conclusions:** Angry people often jump to negative conclusions without adequate evidence for their position. They might assume negative intentions from people without a good reason to make that assumption. When their boss asks them for a meeting, for example, they might jump to the idea that they are going to be given more work.

- **Personalization:** This is when people make events about themselves that are really not about them. They essentially take things personally, assuming that people did things with them in mind. In the case of anger, they might decide that a person's actions were motivated by spite or revenge. "They did that just to get back at me."

All-or-Nothing Thinking

I've been the target of a lot of anger on social media lately because of my position on American gun violence. I'm a staunch and outspoken advocate for increased gun regulation in the United States and I discuss it often on social media.* Something interesting happens when I do this, though, that speaks to a particular thought style common among angry people. Inevitably, gun enthusiasts attack me for wanting to "ban guns" – they say things like, "Good luck taking my guns from me," "If you ban guns only criminals will have them," or even "How about we ban cars too since those kill even more people than guns."

---

* My position on guns is undeniably informed by my research on anger and other emotions. Take any emotionally volatile situation, add a gun to it, and you've certainly made that situation more dangerous.

What makes this such an odd response, though, is that I've never advocated the banning of all guns and I've never talked about confiscating guns. They hear "gun regulation" – which can mean anything from requiring that guns be locked away to requiring additional training to own a gun – and they translate it in their minds into the banning and confiscating of all guns. They end up responding to this idea instead of what I am actually advocating. This is the sort of all-or-nothing thinking that really drives the worldviews of many angry people.

All-or-nothing thinking is when people categorize things as *all bad* or *all good*. They take a situation or an idea and label or define it as being a particular way, failing to account for the nuance within that situation or idea. As I'm writing this, for example, it's pouring down with rain outside and will likely continue for the next few hours. I could define this as terrible or disappointing because it's going to *ruin* my run later and keep my kids from being able to play outside. In doing so, though, I would be ignoring the fact that the rain is feeding my garden that desperately needs the water (not to mention the crops of local farmers). The rain isn't inherently bad. It's just a thing that's happening and has both positive and negative influences on my life and the broader community.

This sort of thinking happens in describing people too. Instead of recognizing human beings as having complex motivations, angry people might label others as *cruel, stupid,* or *dishonest.* Those labels become the lens by which they interpret their behavior. When a person who has been labeled dishonest tries to explain themselves, it is assumed to be a lie. When a person who has been labeled stupid offers a solution to a problem, it is ignored.

Once again, we've been able to identify a variety of thought types that fall into this all-or-nothing category. Here are a few examples of the thoughts we might see from angry people, including examples of how those thoughts might lead to anger:

- **Overgeneralizing:** This is the tendency to broaden experiences out into a much bigger pattern. When a thing happens, they might describe it as *always* happening instead of thinking of it as a single incident. For instance, when a child forgets to do their homework, the angry parent might say, "Why does he *always* do that?" or even "He is *completely* irresponsible."

- **Inflammatory labeling:** This is when they label people or situations in highly negative or even cruel ways. They describe situations as completely terrible or disastrous. They describe people as total idiots, fools, or worthless. In doing so, they fail to realize that people are more complicated than they realize and that their motivations for doing something in a particular moment are similarly complicated.

- **Differing versions of fairness:** Some people evaluate outcomes in terms of fairness, but not in a way that is consistent with how others view fairness. Anger emerges because they feel injustice that others don't necessarily see or agree with. A spouse might, for instance, think "It's only fair that they vacuum since I made dinner" and get angry when their partner doesn't see it the same way.

- **Considering opinions to be facts:** People sometimes misconstrue their own opinions to be facts, meaning they think that because they feel a certain way about something, other people should feel that way too.[*] "I think Casablanca is the best movie of all time" becomes "Casablanca is the best movie of all time" and anger ensues when others don't recognize this as an obvious fact.

---

[*] When my son was nine years old, he got really upset listening to a podcast where some critics disparaged a movie he had really enjoyed. He had loved it and couldn't believe that other people didn't love it too. This is something we expect from children, but we also expect they will grow out of as they develop a more sophisticated understanding of how people experience the world around them.

Disaster Thinking

When we interpret any situation we encounter or any experience we have, we interpret it in two different ways. Initially, we interpret the source itself. In the case of anger, we look to the person or situation we are feeling provoked by and we make decisions about what it means to us. This is where a lot of the thoughts we've already discussed come into play. We're deciding who did what, why they did it, whether or not it was bad or good, how it impacts us, and so on. We call this primary appraisal.

When we're done with this, we decide how bad the situation is for us and whether or not we can cope with it. This is secondary appraisal and it's critical to whether or not we get angry and how angry we might get. There are situations, for instance, where a person behaved badly but where it didn't impact us much, so we might not get as mad. If a person cuts in front of me in line at a coffee shop, I might think "They did that on purpose and it was rude, but I'm not in a hurry so it's not that big a deal." In doing so, I might get a little angry over what they did, thinking it was unfair or disrespectful, but not terribly mad because it had such a small impact on my life. If I think to myself, though, "Now I'm going to be late for work" or "This guy is gonna get the last donut," I will likely get much angrier. My interpretation of the consequences informs my anger.

The angry people in your life probably have a tendency to think catastrophically. In the case of Ephraim above, he found himself particularly frustrated by interruptions because he interpreted them as interfering significantly in his work. It's an interesting situation because he recognized that people weren't doing anything wrong by asking him for help. His job was to help them. So his primary appraisal alone didn't necessarily lead to frustration or anger. He didn't really interpret people as having done anything wrong. Yet his secondary appraisal, where he evaluated his ability to cope with the situation, did lead to anger. It's already hard for him to focus because of his ADHD, so these interruptions are especially disruptive to him.

There are a few different ways that angry people engage in this sort of thinking. First, though, I want to acknowledge that some situations truly are catastrophic. I don't want to minimize the fact people do experience truly negative outcomes. Far from it. What I'm talking about here is a tendency to blow things out of proportion, which is not to deny that sometimes things really are bad and anger, along with other emotions, is reasonable.

- **Catastrophizing:** This is the most obvious and it's captured fairly well by the broader category of disaster thinking. Angry people tend to blow negative events way out of proportion by interpreting the outcome of those events as highly negative. They decide an experience is the worst thing that's ever happened to them or that it is going to ruin their entire day, week, career. When a co-worker forgets to finish a task, for example, the person might say, "Now I'm going to get way behind. My day is ruined."
- **Emotional reasoning:** When people engage in emotional reasoning, they start to believe that their feelings reflect the truth about a given situation. They think that their anger, for instance, must mean that the situation was truly bad, unfair, or unjust. They fail to see that there may be other interpretations of what happened.
- **Filtering/dismissing positives:** This is when people fail to acknowledge positive outcomes in their life in favor of negative ones. They notice the things that are going badly and filter out the positive experiences. So an angry person might get hyper-focused on a particular thing that went wrong one day (a delayed flight, a lost restaurant reservation) and think their day is ruined, while failing to acknowledge the things that went well that day or the fun they had.

ANGER FACT

People with angry personalities are much more likely to experience thoughts in all three of the categories discussed above, to recap: high expectations of others, all-or-nothing thinking, and disaster thinking.[48]

The Origin of Our Worldviews

It's obvious from just glancing at these thought types that they would be associated with anger (not to mention other emotions like sadness and fear). A person who catastrophizes has a tendency to make the bad situations they experience that much worse in their minds in a way that leads to increased anger. A person who overgeneralizes has a tendency to take a particular situation and expand it to be part of a pattern. When their spouse has to work late and spoils their plans, they respond with "They always do this" and they feel extra frustrated. From ignoring the positives to demandingness to inflammatory labeling, it makes intuitive sense that these thought types would lead to anger and aggression.

Indeed, this is confirmed by the research too. Consistently, studies of these thought types have linked them to anger, sadness, and fear. People who have these types of thoughts often aren't just more likely to get mad, they are more likely to express their anger in maladaptive or dangerous ways.[49] These findings have some really important implications for therapy and self-help too, in that we know that these thoughts are where intervention often works best. In keeping with Beck's original ideas, research has confirmed that one of the best ways to help angry people is to help them change these thoughts. When people replace their angering thoughts with more adaptive thoughts, they experience less anger and express it in healthier ways.

To me, though, what is equally fascinating is to consider where these thoughts are learned and developed. Why do some people gravitate toward these particular thought types in the first place? Ephraim said something really important about this when he talked about the origin of his so often feeling misunderstood and devalued. He talked about his mother, who he described as controlling, and how he felt like his feelings and thoughts were devalued throughout his childhood. He felt misunderstood for so much of his life that it has been a consistent source of frustration to him.

Our thought tendencies likely develop through a similar mechanism as our emotion tendencies. We learn some of it through rewards and punishments when our caregivers actively encourage or discourage ways of thinking by praising or scolding us. When a child does poorly on a test and says, "It wasn't my fault. The teacher didn't teach us that stuff" a parent might agree and support them, which acts like a reward. Or they might scold them for externalizing the blame, which acts like a punishment and encourages them to think differently. They may even offer them alternative explanations of what happened or different ways of thinking about the situation.

That said, much of how of our worldview develops likely comes through modeling. We pick up on how our caregivers think of things through the thoughts they actually vocalize during their day-to-day experiences. When one of our parents says, "Look at this idiot" or "This happens every time" or "Well now the entire day is ruined," we take in those interpretations and thinking styles. We start to label people, overgeneralize, and catastrophize because those things have been modeled for us. It's worth noting too, that while our caregivers might be the most influential here early on, it isn't just them. Like our emotions, our worldviews are built through interactions with our siblings, our friends, teachers, the celebrities or leaders we pay attention to, and others.

ACTIVITY: THE THOUGHTS OF OTHERS

Returning once more to that angry person in your life, think again about a time they were really angry, but play close attention to the thoughts they articulated. What did they say that might illustrate what they were thinking?

1. Thinking about the categories of thought described above, what types of thoughts was this person demonstrating?
2. How might those thoughts be reflective of a broader worldview that informs how they see the world?
3. To the degree that you know, what aspects of their development might have influenced or led this worldview?

"Give Me Time"

I thought Ephraim's answer to my question about how people can best interact with him was important and interesting. He said, "To give me time." He's not asking people to bend over backwards for him or to disregard their own feelings in favor of his. He just wants people to give him space and time to work through his own thoughts and feelings before he responds. It took him a little longer to work through change and he wanted people to recognize that and give him that opportunity.

Now, Ephraim struck me as a much more emotionally sensitive and insightful person than most people we might interact with. He also struck me as considerate in ways we don't expect of angry people. He was concerned about the impact his anger was having on others, especially his fiancée. With most angry people in our lives, we might not get that sort of thoughtfulness and dealing effectively with them may require more of us. In Part Two, I tackle ten strategies for effectively dealing with angry people.

PART TWO

TEN STRATEGIES
FOR DEALING WITH
ANGRY PEOPLE

CHAPTER 6

STRATEGY ONE: WORK OUT WHAT YOU REALLY WANT

"If he didn't want to know what I thought, he shouldn't have asked me"

A friend of mine recently told me about a very unpleasant anger-related situation she was having with one of her in-laws. As a family, they were dealing with some complicated health issues that required making some difficult decisions. My friend was asked by her father-in-law what she thought they should do. She was honest with the advice she gave even though she knew he wouldn't like it. What she hadn't anticipated, though, was how much he wouldn't like it and how angry he would become.

He was livid. She received an email from him that was exceedingly angry and hostile. He questioned her commitment to their family and told her she had no right to say such things. When she tried to explain that she was just offering her opinion the way he had asked her to, he attacked her again with a second email. This one was even more aggressive. She decided not to respond to that one and he never followed up with her. At the time she told me all of this, her father-in-law had cut off contact with her and though he was still communicating with her husband, he had become very cold to him. She was hurt and scared about what all this might mean to their family.

On top of the hurt and fear, though, she was also really mad at him. He had asked her opinion, so she provided it. "If he didn't want to know what I thought, he shouldn't have asked me," she told me. "He didn't really want my opinion. He just wanted me to tell him that he was doing the right thing." In retrospect, she wished she hadn't said anything. She wished she had just told him to do what he thought was right and moved on. But now she was in this awful situation where she felt like the only way out was to apologize for something she wasn't really sorry for.

The entire situation brought a lot of deep feelings to the surface for her, and she found herself wanting to tell him things she knew would be unproductive. She was mad, and that anger did what anger often does. She wanted to lash out. At the same time, though, she knew that saying or doing what she wanted to do in this situation wasn't going to get her to her overall goal in the situation. Because what she really wanted was to preserve the relationship between her husband and her father-in-law.

TIP

Finding a way to pause in an emotional moment is one of the most important things you can do to effectively work with angry people.

What We Want to Do vs. What We Should Do

One of the best things we can do when someone is angry with us is figure out what our goals are for the situation. What is the outcome we want and how do we get there? This is applicable in fairly brief interactions like a dispute on the road or in more complex situations like the one above or those involving co-workers, friends, or other family. Before we react, we should give ourselves a chance to pause and assess the situation to decide how we can get to the outcome we want.

In any given situation, there are quite a few different outcomes you may want to seek out. Perhaps, for example, a friend gets angry with you because you decided not to attend a party they were having. At the time they say they are ok with it and understand, but you later learn they have said some hostile things about you to your mutual friends. In a situation like this, there are a number of different outcomes you might want, depending on the nature of your relationship with them. For instance:

- You may want them to stop being mad at you.
- You may want them to stop talking about you with others.
- You may want to end the friendship.
- You may want to alleviate your own guilt over not going.
- You may want to preserve your reputation with others.
- You may want to get back at them.

Each of these goals might require a different response from you, and to make things even more complicated, you might want to accomplish more than one of these things.

Taking time in these moments to think about your desired outcome can be really difficult. By definition, these are emotionally charged situations and we're not always thinking clearly. What we *want* to do in these situations might be different from what we *need* to do to get to the outcome we desire. Instead of focusing on our goals, we often focus instead on getting back at the person. We follow our knee-jerk reaction for revenge, instead of slowing down and being strategic. There is a reason for this instinct, by the way, and like a lot of things related to our emotions, it's rooted deep in our DNA.

An Instinct for Revenge

I was recently talking about anger on social media and someone responded to a post with a really fascinating and insightful comment about how hard it can be for them to let things go when they are confronted by an angry person. They said that trying to walk away in those situations left them feeling emasculated, so they would end up lashing out even though they knew it wasn't the best thing to do. This comment was interesting on its own, but what was equally fascinating was all the other readers who agreed with this person. There was this very clear, shared understanding that one of the things that prevents people from making a good choice in these emotionally charged situations was the feeling that if they didn't fight back, they were being taken advantage of.

ANGER FACT

Getting revenge activates the parts of our brain associated with rewards.

So why is this desire for revenge so powerful? What is it about getting back at someone that motivates us to do something that runs contrary to our goals? In 2004, a team of researchers explored just that, specifically looking at what happens in our brains when we get revenge.[50] They scanned the brains of participants who were playing a game, anonymously, against another participant. The game involved exchanges of money where if the participants were honest and worked together, they could both benefit. However, if one was willing to take advantage of the other, that person could benefit even more. Essentially, if someone wanted to behave dishonorably and trick the other participant, they could try to do so and potentially make more money that way.

However, the person who was taken advantage of in the study was later given the opportunity to get revenge. Once they had found out they had been tricked, they were given a minute to decide if they wanted to punish the person by taking away points in the game they were playing. During that minute while they were deciding, their brains were being studied via a PET scan.* What they found was that the act of punishing the person who had wronged them led to activation of a brain structure called the dorsal striatum. The dorsal striatum plays a really important role in responsiveness to rewards, so the authors argue that "activations in the dorsal striatum reflect expected satisfaction." In other words, the desire to punish wasn't just something they saw as the right thing to do, they enjoyed it. Assigning the punishment gave them pleasure.

This says a lot about how difficult it is to walk away in these moments. Our drive for revenge is very strong.† It is rewarding to get back at people. Like other emotion-related experiences, it is likely rooted in our evolutionary history. It was in our ancestors' best interest to respond when provoked or wronged, as it sent a clear message to anyone who might try and harm them or attempt to take their resources: Don't mess with me. It gives us pleasure now because our ancestors, human and nonhuman, who were more likely to get revenge (which they did because it felt good), were more likely to survive.

At the same time, though, it's been well established that even though revenge feels good in the moment, it often doesn't feel good later on. After getting revenge, people tend to get stuck thinking about those negative feelings. They continue to ruminate about the situation. There's a fascinating study from 2008 that explored this question in detail.[51] Similar to the study above, they had participants play a game. They embedded a fake participant into the study, though, who would essentially double-cross the real participants in a way that angered them and left them wanting revenge. Half of the real participants got the opportunity for revenge and the other half did not. After

* PET stands for Positron Emission Tomography and it involves injecting a tracer into the body that is then picked up by the scan. It's typically used to identify cancers, brain disorders, heart problems, and other disorders.
† In fact, research on the dorsal striatum finds that it is involved with the development of addictive behaviors. While it would be going too far to say that revenge can be addictive, this illustrates how intense the desire for revenge might be for some people.

that part of the study was over, participants got a survey to assess their mood.

There are two really interesting findings here. First, the group that didn't get revenge really wished they had been given the opportunity to get revenge. That speaks to the drive for revenge I've been describing. If they couldn't get revenge, they were disappointed. Second, and this is surprising and important, the group that didn't get revenge was happier after the study than the group that got revenge. Tthey didn't know they were happier than the other group and thought they would be happiest if they had the chance to get revenge, but they were actually happier without it. In other words, we're most likely better off if we fight the urge to respond immediately when people treat us badly.

Avoiding Revenge for a Better Outcome

Let's run through some examples of where we might be inclined to seek revenge instead of working toward a better, more thoughtful goal. Below we consider how to avoid revenge online, at the office, and at home.

Online

Imagine you are on social media and you comment on a friend's political post. Someone you have never met before – a friend of your friend – responds to you with an angry and even aggressive and insulting post. Most of us probably don't have to imagine this – you can just think back to a time when this very thing has happened to you. In fact, data from The Anger Project reveals that 23 per cent of people get into online arguments at least once a month.[52] In that moment, you might feel the desire to fire back at them – to really let them have it for insulting you. But if you stop and think through your goals in this situation, you may come to a completely different course of action.

For instance, you may decide your goal isn't to get revenge. You may decide you don't want to insult them or try to prove them wrong. Rather, your goal might be to convince anyone reading the thread of your position, and you write a response intended for that broader audience. That could entail an entirely different tone or approach. Instead of the hostility you might have started with, you shift to a positive approach that is more likely to resonate with other readers. Or you may decide that your goal is to preserve your relationship with your friend – the original poster. In that case, maybe you don't respond at all for worry that this stranger and your friend are close and preserving a relationship with your friend might mean that you shouldn't insult or attack someone on the social-media feed.

At the Office

Now imagine you make a mistake at your job that causes one of your co-workers some extra work and some understood frustration. That co-worker responds with a very hostile email to you about the mistake you made and the time it cost them. You understandably get defensive and maybe even a little angry yourself. People often tell me that their gut reaction to situations like this – likely rooted in defensiveness – is to fire back in a similarly hostile way. Rather than admit the mistake or offer an apology, they try to turn the cause back on the person with a "I know I made a mistake but…" or "It wouldn't have happened if you hadn't…."

It's natural and understandable to get defensive when someone is angry with you. In fact, it would be weird *not* to want to defend yourself in such situations. It would really run contrary to our nature. That said, this is clearly one of those cases where identifying your goals is critical to your success. It's also contextual, meaning there are a number of complicated relationship factors at play (such as, is this person a supervisor or can they otherwise harm your career progression?). In the end, to navigate such a moment, you need to think about what you want to get out of this situation. Do you want to repair the relationship, solve the problem you created, let them know they shouldn't communicate in such a hostile way, or maybe all of those things? Once again, we find that taking a moment to think through our goals is necessary to navigating these situations successfully.

At Home

One type of situation where this drive for revenge is particularly complicated is with parents and their children. Few parents would use the word "revenge" to describe their parenting approach, but listening to the way parents talk about their use of punishment often reveals justice-related motivations rather than educational or developmental motivations. When I have talked to parents about their use of punishments, including physical punishments like spanking, they often offer explanations that sound an awful lot like revenge. Parents routinely say things to me like, "Well they deserved a punishment" or even that their kids "had it coming." Frankly, a number of people have told me that they were spanked as children because they "deserved it."*

Yet this line of thinking doesn't typically get parents what they want, which is to curb the problematic behavior. Take, for instance, a situation where a child gets angry at a sibling and expresses that anger in the way many young children do, by hitting. Parents routinely respond to this sort of behavior through a combination of scolding, punishment, or even spanking† (often using the justice/revenge rationale to support it). Instead, parents should pause to think about their desired outcome. What do you really want in this moment? Usually, the answer to that question is (or at least it should be) to help the child find different ways to express their anger. That outcome requires a very different path than scolding or punishment.

It requires modeling, support, and the teaching of adaptive coping strategies. Start, then, by modeling healthy anger expressions.

---

* "Some kids deserve to be hit. Deal with it." I was once told by a follower on TikTok.

† A 2017 study in *JAMA Pediatrics* found that while the prevalence of spanking children has declined in the United States, more than one-third of parents still do it. This is despite a wealth of data finding that spanking isn't just ineffective, it actually leads to many of the outcomes parents are trying to prevent (dishonesty, aggression, and other conduct problems).

Speak with them in the voice you would want them to use when they are angry (calm, firm). Encourage them to think about why they are angry and what they can do about it. Empathize with the feelings they are experiencing while also offering them other ways of dealing with those feelings, such as deep breathing, taking time to themselves, and assertiveness. If the goal is for them to express their anger in a healthier and more appropriate way, your response should be about helping them achieve that goal.

Three Steps to Identifying Your Goals

You can break down the process into three steps: (1) pause, (2) collect your thoughts and ask yourself what you want to achieve, and (3) determine how to get there.

Step One: Find a way to pause

The most difficult part of identifying your goals is taking the time to actually do it. It requires that you stop yourself from reacting immediately, and potentially poorly, and find time to think through the situation and what you want from it. When you react too quickly to another's anger, you may start down a path that is difficult to come back from. Instead, find a way to pause in those moments.

This is something I'm going to spend the entire next chapter on, so know that there's a lot more information coming. In the meantime, though, here are a few suggestions to help you find a way to pause. First, understand that you have to be intentional about it as a life strategy. It takes far more psychological effort to stay calm than to act so you need to prepare yourself in advance. Second, get in the habit of counting slowly to three, taking a deep breath and exhaling,* or even shaking out your shoulders the way you might after exercising.

---

* As a longtime zombie movie enthusiast, I often let out a zombie noise in these moments. This has the dual effect of giving me a moment to pause and also making me and those around me laugh. I wish I could say it was an intentional strategy. It wasn't. I just discovered myself doing it one day.

Step Two: Ask yourself, "What do I want to get out of this situation?"

Once you've had a moment to collect yourself, start thinking about the ideal outcome for this situation. What do you want for the parties involved, including yourself? Don't trouble yourself yet with what is reasonable or likely or even what the other person "deserves" in this circumstance. Those things are just distractions at this point. Ask yourself what you want and stay focused on that.

Step Three: Ask yourself, "What is the best route to obtain that outcome?"

Finally, start thinking about the best route to obtain that goal. When my friend decided she wanted to preserve the relationship between her husband and her father-in-law, the next step was to determine the best way to do that. If you decided you want to preserve your relationship with the person that is mad at you, then start thinking about how to repair that relationship in a meaningful way. If you decide that your goal is to help your kids learn to manage their anger in ways other than hitting, then focus your energies away from justice and more toward teaching and support.

Staying Calm in Emotional Times

Of course, you won't be able to do any of this unless you learn to stay calm yourself. The capacity for rational, goal-oriented thought is built on your ability to quickly de-escalate yourself in these emotional moments. As you've already learned, this ability is rooted in your biology and your developmental history. It's connected to your worldview and influenced by what is going on in your environment during the emotional moment itself. At the same time, though, the ability to say calm is a skill, one that can be honed through practice and effort. In the next chapter, we'll go further into how to keep your cool.

CHAPTER 7
STRATEGY TWO: KEEP YOUR COOL

A Sweaty, Shaky, Breathy, Red Mess

There are two questions I get almost every time I do an interview or speak with a group about anger. First: Are people angrier than we used to be?* Second: How do I stay calm in the moment when I'm angry? This second one is a really important question, and frankly, it can be extended outside of anger to any emotionally charged moment. When someone is angry with you – or even not angry *with you* but with someone else around you – how do you keep your cool?

The first step in understanding what you need to do to stay calm in these situations is understanding what is going on in your body in these moments. When you have strong emotions, part of what is happening is that your sympathetic nervous system – often called your fight-or-flight system – kicks in. This is one of the ways your body protects itself from danger or responds to a threat. Your brain prepares your body for a fight, if necessary, or to flee, by increasing your heart rate and breathing rate. Epinephrine is released into your system, giving you extra energy. That extra energy might increase your body temperature, make your face red, or even make your hands shake. You might start to sweat to cool yourself off. Because digestion is relatively unimportant in a crisis, your digestive system slows down, which means you stop salivating. Your mouth goes dry, making it harder for you to talk.

---

* There's really no way to answer this one. We don't have a consistent mechanism to track this sort of thing over time. My best guess is that, in some ways, we are angrier than we used to be, but that we're also witnessing that anger in new ways because of the omnipresence of social media and video. Public displays of anger that used to be invisible to us are now much more evident.

In other words, when you have strong emotions, you become a sweaty, shaky, breathy, red mess with a dry mouth and an elevated heart rate. Trying to communicate in those moments is like trying to talk to someone after you've run a 100-meter-dash at full pace. It's hard to think clearly and it's even harder to formulate the words that will best get you where you want to be in a situation like this.

Typically, it takes about 20 minutes to fully recover from this fight-or-flight state. Not 20 minutes from the start of the elevation, but 20 minutes after the stressful situation has passed. The activity of the sympathetic nervous system is pretty much automatic, so efforts to prevent it are fairly futile. What we are going to cover here, though, is twofold. First, how can you decrease that time from 20 minutes to something more manageable. Second, and more importantly, how can we continue to communicate effectively and conduct ourselves in a healthy way even when we're in this elevated state.

What Not To Do

Let's start, though, with what not to do. A common claim is that a way to "release" our emotions in these moments is to punch things, break things, scream, or even exercise.* This is such a common claim, in fact, that "rage rooms" have cropped up across the world as places for people to go and work through their anger by breaking things. The one nearest where I live, for example, offers a place "when you've had a long day, hour, month or year." They describe it as a space to "break things to your own music and in your own way."†

---

* When I ask people, "What are you releasing in these moments?" they often say, "the anger." But what does that mean? Anger isn't a gas. It's not a thing we can release into the atmosphere.

† They also describe themselves as "available for gender reveal parties?" This can't be a thing, right? People are not going to rage rooms for gender reveals, right?

ANGER FACT

"Releasing" your anger by punching things, breaking things, or screaming actually increases anger instead of decreasing it.

It is a well-established fact that this approach to anger reduction doesn't work. It might feel good in the moment* but it does not help alleviate those negative emotions. In fact, study after study reveals that such approaches make our emotions worse in the long run. People who use catharsis to deal with negative emotions are more aggressive after that catharsis and more likely to want to harm.

The same goes for exercise, which is often surprising to people. Here, though, the devil is in the details. Exercise is good for your emotional wellbeing overall. That is well established. People who exercise regularly have a healthier emotional life. Exercise improves mood and helps people manage their anxiety. But that doesn't mean you should exercise during an emotional episode or as a way to calm down from an emotional episode. When you are in the midst of an emotional experience (such as anger, fear, even intense sadness), exercise can exacerbate those negative feelings through something called excitation transfer.

Excitation transfer is the finding that emotions are intensified by arousal not associated with them. Essentially, the excitation (elevated heart rate, increased breathing) from one experience *transfers* to another experience, so if you're angry, and you go for a run, your heart rate will increase because of the run, but your brain will think it's because you're angry. Researchers have known this for the past 50 years, ever since Dr. Dolf Zillmann

---

* So does using alcohol and overeating by the way. But that doesn't make those things good for you.

and colleagues did the 1972 study, "Excitation transfer from physical exercise to subsequent aggressive behavior."[53] Like almost every study on anger and aggression from the 1970s, they provoked their participants first to get them good and mad. Then participants were randomly assigned to either ride an exercise bike or engage in a mundane task.* When they were done, they got to respond to the person who provoked them. If exercise were effective in reducing anger, they would be less aggressive after riding the bike. But they weren't, they were more aggressive.

These findings, though, haven't necessarily moved the needle on therapists' recommendations to people when angry. A quick internet search of "how do I calm down when I'm angry?" yields pages of results advocating punching bags, rage rooms, and exercise. Meanwhile, I routinely talk with people who tell me their therapists encourage them to work out when they get mad or to have their children punch a pillow when they are angry. For whatever reason, we haven't been able to effectively get the word out on the harm that can come from catharsis.

Shortening That 20 Minutes

So if a lot of people's go-to for calming down, catharsis/exercise, isn't good for them, what does work? What are some ways that people can stay calm in these emotionally charged situations?

Make it a Core Value

Most important, you need to embrace the desire to stay calm in these situations as an intentional life strategy. It is exceedingly difficult in the moment to *decide* you want to stay calm. Everything about the situation is screaming for you to emote, so deciding not to in the midst of the actual situation is nearly

---

* The mundane task "consisted of the continuous 'blind' threading of nickel-sized discs with off-center holes." Somehow, this mind-numbingly boring task made participants less angry than riding a stationary bike.

impossible. For this reason, you should make the decision to stay calm in advance of the situation.

What I mean here is that if you think of yourself as a person who wants to stay calm in these situations (better yet, a person who *does* stay calm in these situations), then there is no longer a decision to make when it happens to you. You've already made it and what you need to do at that point is simply work on being the person you have already said you want to be.

This may sound a little too simple, so try and think about it this way. It's about habit forming, and the hardest part about creating new habits is avoiding falling back on old habits during times of tension. Imagine you are trying to eat healthier foods (more vegetables, less sugar, and so on) and you go out to a restaurant for dinner. If you try and decide on the spot what to have, in the midst of all those tantalizing options, you are more likely to fall back on old habits. But if you look at the online menu and make your decisions in advance of getting to the restaurant, prior to being surrounded by temptation, you are more likely to make the healthy choice in the moment. Similarly, if you make the decision in advance to stay calm when faced by another's anger, you have that to fall back on when things get heated.

Find (or Create) a Pause

Even if you've decided you want to be (or are) the type of person who stays calm in these moments, it can still be exceptionally difficult to catch yourself when you start to escalate. When someone gets angry with you and you start to match that anger with your own escalated emotion, it can be easy to forget your intention to remain calm. One strategy for dealing with this is to identify a "pause button" in your mind. As soon as you become aware of your escalation, make an effort to remind yourself of who you want to be in these moments. Pause, even if it means ignoring the person you are interacting with for a moment, to find some inner peace before you continue.

I realize that this is easier said than done, but it can happen with practice. Later in the chapter, I'll address some strategies for how to engage in that practice. But for now, understand that to stay calm, you must be able to identify in the emotional moment a time to pause and de-escalate.

TIP

Deep breathing is the cornerstone of any in-the-moment attempt to stay calm.

Deep Breathing

There is a wonderful video floating around social media right now of a six-year-old helping his four-year-old brother calm down with some breathing exercises. The description says that the younger brother was about to have a tantrum and his older brother was helping him work through it. It is adorable (and it nicely shows off that modeling we talked about in chapter 3).* It is also just a perfect example of how we can use deep breathing to calm ourselves down.

There are two parts of your autonomic nervous system: the parasympathetic (sometimes referred to as "rest and digest") and the sympathetic nervous system (the "fight-or-flight" system referenced above). When you get angry, the fight-or-flight system activates and the parasympathetic nervous system shuts down. Another way of saying this is that you can't be emotionally escalated (scared, angry, surprised) and relaxed at the same time. These are what we refer to as *incongruent mood states*. This also

---

* Maybe this is the kind of big brother Floyd Allport was? Maybe my assumption that he just tortured his younger brother into giving him first authorship says more about me than it does him?

means that the way to shut down the fight-or-flight system is to activate the rest-and-digest system, and one of the ways you can do that is through deep breathing.

Deep breathing can look a lot of different ways. In fact, I couldn't possibly provide an all-inclusive list right now. Instead, I'll share three popular strategies: box, triangle, and 4-7-8. With box breathing, you engage in a four count while you inhale, hold, exhale, hold, and repeat. In other words, you count to four while inhaling, count to four while holding your breath, count to four while exhaling, and count to four while holding your lungs empty, and continue this for a minute or so.

Triangle breathing is very similar to this approach with one small difference. Instead of holding with your lungs empty, you skip that part (so it's a triangle instead of a box). You count to four while breathing in, hold for a four count, and breath out for a four count. Then repeat.

Finally, with 4-7-8 breathing, you lay your tongue against the roof of your mouth and keep it there throughout the exercise. You breath all the air out of your lungs (making a whooshing sound as the air passes by your tongue through your mostly closed mouth). You then inhale quietly through your nose for a four count. Then, you hold your breath for a count to seven. Finally, you exhale for an eight count, again making the whooshing sound as the air passes by your tongue. You repeat this for a minute or so.

As you have likely gathered from this, the key here is not so much that one of these is better than the other, but that you find something that works for you. The principles behind all three of these exercises (and pretty much all other breathing exercises) is to take long, slow, deep breaths where you draw attention to your lungs and focus on your breathing. In doing so, you start to deactivate the response of the sympathetic nervous system and feel calm.

Relax Your Body

Of course, deep breathing isn't the only way to relax your body. It is relatively critical in that a deep breath should be included in any attempt to calm down in the moment, but there are other options available to you along with it. One other strategy here is to do some intentional muscle relaxation.

Progressive muscle relaxation is an often-used approach to relaxation, especially as a treatment for various anxiety disorders. Using the same principle as with deep breathing, the goal is to activate the parasympathetic nervous system as a way of countering the fight-or-flight system. The approach typically involves tensing a specific set of muscles in part of your body, holding it for a few seconds, and then relaxing those muscles. In doing so, you experience an increased sense of relaxation in that muscle group. Progressive muscle relaxation is when you do this progressively, moving from muscle group to muscle group throughout the body, and start to feel that sense of relaxation across the body.

Obviously, though, in an emotional moment, like when someone is angry with you, you don't have the opportunity to go through a progressive muscle relaxation routine. You can, however, take a moment to tense up your body intentionally for a few seconds with the goal of feeling that sense of relaxation when you release.

Take a Moment to Ground Yourself

Grounding is the psychological process of bringing ourselves back to a state of peace and relaxation. In some ways, you can think of it as finding equilibrium, a state where you feel psychologically comfortable. There are different ways to ground yourself, including some of the things I've already discussed like deep breathing or progressive muscle relaxation. Other popular options include taking a walk, holding a piece of ice, submerging your hands in water, or even just carrying a grounding object around with you like a small stone you like to rub between your fingers. Some of these options, though, are difficult to do in that emotional moment. In those cases, I find the 5-4-3-2-1 method to be particularly helpful.

This method includes taking a moment to identify five things you can see, four things you can touch, three things you can hear, two things you can smell, and one thing you can taste. So in an emotional moment when you are feeling anxious, tense, or even angry, you can take a moment to look around you in an effort to ground yourself and lessen that emotional feeling. By the time you get to the one thing you can taste, you should have a greater sense of calm and control.

Have a Mantra

In emotionally charged moments, having a mantra can be a really effective way to calm yourself. It's easy to feel like a situation is getting out of control when a person is angry with you. Your thoughts might start to feel a little scattered and you may have a difficult time focusing. A mantra or affirmation – something you say to yourself internally – can help you take back some power and sense of control in these moments by reminding you that you are capable of getting through this. For instance, any of the following statements can be valuable in moments like these:

- I'm strong enough for this.
- I have control of myself right now.
- I can handle this.
- This situation is temporary.
- I am _____ in these moments [patient, kind, strong, for instance].

You can think of such mantras as a combination of encouragement, meaning-making, and even some planning. By telling yourself that you have control right now, you are both encouraging yourself to hang in there and also reminding yourself that staying in control is important. It is both inspirational and practical.

> **TIP**
>
> Take a moment to identify a mantra that will work for you in these moments. You may even have a specific mantra for specific situations where you anticipate you're going to interact with an angry person.

Putting These All Together

Ultimately, none of these tools are going to work on their own all of the time. It's not so much that the tool itself is imperfect, but that situations vary in such ways that you can't rely on just one particular go-to approach. There may, for instance, be times when grounding is just not effective for you because you're so emotional that you can't adequately find your center. In those moments, perhaps deep breathing or relaxing your muscles is more effective. The other issue here, though, is that the best approach is likely something that will include multiple strategies.

I would argue that one of the best things you can do when faced with an emotional moment is to follow through with a relatively quick and standard progression. As soon as you can, find your moment to pause and collect yourself. Then, take a deep breath, shake out your muscles, and center yourself, as you try to think through your goals and next options. Of course, it might not be possible to do all these things in the moment, given the speed with which these emotional incidents can happen, but the progression I just described can happen in just a few seconds, and can result in a clearer head when it is through.

Planning and Rehearsing

Some of the work to stay calm should be done, not in the emotional moment itself, but in advance of the moment and even after the moment has passed. I liken this to an athlete coming up with a strategy in advance of a match or reviewing game film after it's over. We can sometimes plan for these emotional events before they happen and we can certainly reflect on them honestly when they are finished.

Prepare Yourself in Advance

I mentioned earlier how part of staying calm when people are angry with us is deciding what kind of person we want to be. It's deciding how we think of ourselves and living those goals in the moment. But we can be even more intentional than that around specific situations. While many of the situations when you must deal with angry people are unexpected, there are others that you can anticipate and plan for – when you make a decision at work that effects someone negatively, when you tell one of your children something you know will anger them, or just when you are interacting with someone who has a higher propensity for anger. These are all moments where anger is not just possible, but likely. And because it's likely, you can plan for it. You can enter into these situations expecting them to be emotionally charged, and make decisions about how you will handle your emotions.

For instance, imagine you need to tell a co-worker you weren't able to finish a project when you said you would. It's largely your fault. You wanted to get it done, but you were caught up with other responsibilities and it didn't happen. You know this co-worker well enough to know that they will get angry. Maybe because they tend to be cruel or hostile, or maybe because they just tend to take their work seriously, and this will let them down. Because you know this about them, you can plan ahead for their frustration. You can consider the best ways to share the bad news with them. You can identify ways you might solve the problems you have created through this let down. You can even practice for how you will attempt to stay calm when and if they do become angry. Such planning will allow you to feel more in control in the actual emotional moment.

Reflect on it Later

One of the single best ways to learn to stay calm in an emotionally charged moment is to take time to reflect on it later. Even more specifically, reflect on the things *you* did in that moment and how you *could* have handled it. I realize that this may sound odd. How does thinking about the situation after the fact help you stay calm? This is why I compare it to an athlete watching film of a game after a performance. By studying what you did, you can make meaningful changes for the future. You can think about how you want to handle similar situations next time. You can explore the exact moment you *should* have taken a pause, when you wish you had taken a deep breath, or how you could have grounded yourself. All of these thoughts will help you manage your emotions next time.

I was recently talking with someone who said they find themselves thinking back on these situations all the time, but that it rarely feels helpful to them. This person said that they find themself getting emotional all over again. They said they feel like they are reliving the experience and getting all worked up a second (or third or fourth) time.

I have two thoughts on this. First, it's ok to get emotional about it later. In fact, it can even be a good thing because it allows you to practice the calming-down strategies I've been describing. If you find yourself getting worked up in these moments, take a moment to run through the progression above. Find your pause, take a breath, relax your muscles, try to ground yourself.

Second, a mistake many people make in these moments is being overly focused on what the other person did. This sort of rumination is really common. People get caught up in "can you believe they did that" instead of spending time thinking about their own contributions to the situation and how they responded to the person. In keeping with the game film analogy, it is like watching game tape, but only of the other team. You want to spend time thinking about and analyzing the entire situation, and that includes your role in things.

They Don't All Yell and Swear

Of course, for these emotionally charged moments to happen, we have to recognize that people are angry with us in the first place. That is not always the case. People do not always know when someone is mad at them, and that is because not everyone who is angry behaves in a way that looks like the stereotypical angry person. They don't all yell and swear. In the next chapter, we'll talk about how anger can look a lot of different ways.

CHAPTER 8

STRATEGY THREE: REMEMBER THAT ANGER CAN LOOK A LOT OF WAYS

No Yelling, No Lashing Out

I spoke with someone recently about the relationship challenges he was experiencing that stemmed in part from how his wife tended to express her anger. Unlike a lot of the examples I've shared so far, she didn't yell or scream when she was mad. She didn't punch things. She didn't lash out with hurtful comments or even passive-aggressive comments the way many people do. No. When she was angry, she cried.

Usually, these frustration-induced tears weren't directed at him or the result of anything he had done. She would get angry over an inconvenience and would start to cry as a result. Or she would have a disagreement with someone at work and would have a hard time holding back the tears. But sometimes these tears actually *were* the result of an argument between the two of them. At first when this happened, he told me, "I would feel terrible, like I had done something wrong to hurt her."

But over time, he started to feel resentful. "It feels like I can't disagree with her anymore, because she'll start to cry as soon as I do." The pattern was pretty simple. They would disagree about something relatively minor, he would try and talk about it, she would start to cry, and he would feel guilty for making her sad. He ended up feeling pressure to keep his differences to himself for fear of making her cry.

What was so difficult about this dynamic, though, was that she knew she had this tendency, didn't like it about herself, but simply couldn't stop herself in the moment. At the same time that he was feeling resentful, she was feeling embarrassed and guilty. A big part of the problem for him, though, was that he wasn't recognizing these tears as reflecting her anger and frustration. He thought of them as reflecting sadness, so when she cried he immediately gravitated to, "I've made her sad."

Crying is actually a really common, though not often discussed, way that people express their anger. There are a lot of explanations for it, including anger's link to sadness, the feeling of powerlessness that is often at the core of both sadness and frustration, and others. But more than anything, it speaks to something really important about anger and it's that it can be expressed in a number of different ways and some of those ways are not easily recognized as anger.

ANGER FACT

More than 90 per cent of survey respondents said they experienced another negative emotion, such as sadness or fear, as a result of their anger in the past month.[54]

Out, In, and Control

When I first started studying anger, I used a test called the Anger Expression Inventory[55] that measured four types of anger expression: Anger Expression-Out, Anger Expression-In, Anger Control-Out, and Anger Control-In. Anger Expression-Out are those behaviors people typically think of as related to anger. Things like yelling, swearing, slamming doors, and punching things. Anger Expression-In is what we often call anger suppression. It includes holding things in, pouting, and sulking. While there are two types of Anger Control, Out and In, I have always combined them because they don't feel demonstrably different from one another. Technically, Anger Control-Out includes intention efforts to control your behavior by not acting on the anger, and Anger Control-In includes strategies like deep breathing or finding other ways to relax.

At the time, I liked how simple this was, but I quickly discovered that it was too simple. People express their anger in a lot of different ways and these three or four categories just don't cover it meaningfully enough. Some people play or listen to music when they get angry. Others write poetry. Some people find a good friend they can vent to or ask advice of, and others take to the internet to tell the world how angry they are.

And beyond all this, there are all sorts of ways of thinking about angering events that differ in these moments, and these different ways of thinking lead to different ways of acting. A person who gets angry and begins catastrophizing ("This is going to ruin my day") will express and manage their anger differently than someone who starts to refocus on the positive things in their life ("It could be worse"). These different thought types lead to different behaviors and this means that the angry people in our lives will look very different to us in the moment.

Common Expressions of Anger

Let's break down some of the most common ways of behaving when you are angry.

Physical or Verbal Aggression

Physical and verbal aggression is what anger seems most known for. Some people express their anger by trying to harm someone or something either through physical means (hitting, pushing, shooting) or through abusive and cruel statements. They might give someone the finger while driving or scream obscenities at someone who slowed them down. This might also include a person who throws their remote at their television after their team loses a game or who slams a door and punches a wall. In these cases, it might not be that there was an intent to break something. Rather it was just an physically expressive approach to showing that anger.

Even these outward aggressive expressions, though, can look differently than people think. Anger-motivated aggression isn't always direct. Sometimes people express their anger by trying to harm others indirectly through spreading rumors about them or intentionally failing to do something they said they would do (for example, what is often called "passive aggression"). Such indirect expressions of anger can look wildly different from the other forms of physical and verbal aggression.

Sulking or Withdrawal

Perhaps the opposite of physical and verbal aggression are those people who express their anger by withdrawing from others or even going off to pout. This is something you might see in people who are deeply avoidant of conflict. They feel angry but because they don't feel comfortable expressing that anger, even in a positive and prosocial way, they withdraw from people, especially those they are angry with. They might go off to be alone, sit in their room and mope, or go for a drive.

TIP

Some people who choose to withdraw when they are angry really just want some time to be on their own. Try to find the balance between letting them know you're available when they are ready and being pushy.

Sometimes, though, sulking or withdrawing from people can be more calculated and manipulative. It isn't the result of conflict discomfort, but rather a mechanism they use to influence the people around them. They go off to pout as a way of trying to control people, essentially signaling "you need to put effort into repairing the damage you've done." For them, it's another way of fighting back and getting revenge that doesn't include throwing punches or hurling insults.

Suppression

Slightly different from sulking or withdrawal, there are some who simply deny their anger feelings… maybe even to themselves. They might tell you they are "fine" despite some very real feelings of frustration and irritation. On the Anger Expression Inventory I mentioned earlier, this type of expression style, called Anger Expression-In, is measured through items like, "I boil inside, but I don't show it" or "I tend to harbor grudges that I don't tell anyone about."

This sort of anger suppression might be invisible to the people around them. It isn't quite the same as the pouting or withdrawal mentioned before because with those forms of anger there might be an acknowledgement of the anger, but an unwillingness to talk about it. The person is essentially saying, "I'm mad, but don't want to talk about it and would prefer to be alone." Here, though, the person simply doesn't share that they are angry. They won't acknowledge their anger to you even if you ask. So you may know or believe them to be angry, but they won't admit it.

Sarcasm

Dr. Clifford Lazarus, a well-known and respected clinical and health psychologist, once said "sarcasm is actually hostility disguised as humor."[56] While I'm not sure this is always the case, there is definitely some truth here. Sarcasm can indeed be motivated by anger in that people will use it to deal with mild or major frustrations they experience. Their computer crashes and they respond with "Well that's just great." Someone asks if they need help with something that they are obviously struggling with and they respond with "No, I'm really enjoying this."

Sarcasm isn't likely intended to be hostile. In fact, it might be a way of making light of the very real pain they are suffering. Like a lot of humor, sarcasm might exist as a way of lightening mood and making social interactions more pleasant. When something bad happens to them, instead of acknowledging the frustration and disappointment directly, they might say, "So that's nice" or "Isn't that just perfect." It can also, though, be a semi-aggressive way of communicating with people. People will use sarcasm as a way of expressing their disappointment in someone. For instance, if they warned someone at work of a potential problem and were ignored, they might say "What a surprise" when that problem actually occurs. In moments like these, the sarcasm exists as a passive-aggressive way of saying "I told you so."

Diffusion

Sometimes people channel their anger into other, often healthy, activities like playing music or writing. They may pour the energy from their anger into their work or a hobby they have. Using diffusion like this can look a few different ways. It can be a strategy for keeping busy and distracting yourself. People will use this activity as a way of thinking about something different than the anger situation instead of focusing on the thing they are angry about. They may play video games, go for a walk, or clean the house.*

Alternatively, it can be a way for people to work through the angry feelings. They may write in their journal about the angering incident as a way of processing their anger. They may write poetry or create art about how they are feeling in

---

* I once asked my students what they do when they are angry. Right out of the gate, a student raised his hand and said, "Knitting!" I can see how this would be a good way to diffuse anger, in that it's good, focused, and calm work. That said, I think there's also a high potential for stabbing.

that moment. Such ways of expressing aren't so much about distraction but about trying to better understand and cope with the angry feelings. There can, of course, be a fine line between writing to understand and writing an aggressive rant where the intent isn't to process the feelings but simply to vent about them. The former can be valuable and therapeutic, while the latter can be unhealthy.

Assertiveness

There are, of course, ways to express anger directly to the person who wronged you that don't include aggression or hostility. Many people express their anger in ways that are assertive. They express their anger toward the person they are angry with in a way that is direct, confident, and honest while not intending to harm them. Such expressions are devoid of insults or intentional cruelty. They don't include character assaults or attempt revenge. They don't overgeneralize to make it about something more than the specific situation. Rather, they are intended to help resolve the problems in a way that minimizes conflict.

TIP

Try not to mistake assertiveness for aggression. A person who is angry with you might share that with you in a way that is not intended to be harmful (assertiveness) and that's very different from someone who tries to hurt you verbally or physically when they are angry (aggression).

Anger-motivated assertiveness is relatively rare. This is largely because it's really difficult for people to be assertive when they are angry. The emotion of anger often includes the desire to lash out at people, so being able to take a step back and express that anger in a way that is direct but doesn't intend harm is a real skill. It is a talent that most people don't have. That said, there are people who can do it and their anger is often unrecognized by those around them. Because of their ability to remain calm and direct without yelling or swearing, people don't view them as angry in those moments. In the spirit of remembering that anger can look a lot of different ways, we need to remember that just because a person is calm on the outside, doesn't mean they are calm on the inside.

Deep Breathing or Relaxation

When my youngest son, currently 11 years old, starts to become angry, the first thing he does is put his arms down at his sides, lowers his shoulders, stares straight ahead, and takes a deep breath. In those moments, it seems like he's tuning everything else around him out and just focusing on staying calm. As described in the previous chapter, this is one of the ways anger can look in people. They experience a provocation, they start to feel angry, and they quickly move to try and calm themselves through deep breathing or some other form of relaxation.

This can happen for a few different reasons. First, it might be an intentional effort like I've described already to stay calm as a way that better serves the interaction. They are angry, but are actively working to interact with you in a healthy and nonaggressive or non-hostile way. Second, for some people, they work to stay calm this way not because they think it will lead to a better outcome, but because they are uncomfortable or even scared of their angry feelings. The anger is upsetting to them so they work to minimize it in the moment.

Exercising or Catharsis

As discussed in the previous chapter, what is easily the most frequent misconception out there about anger is that expressing it through aggression in a "safe way" is a good way to release it. Despite 50 years' worth of research debunking this idea, people routinely tell me this is their go-to approach for dealing with unwanted anger. When they are feeling angry, they make a point of getting to a "safe place" where they can punch a pillow or a punching bag as a way of dealing with that rage.

A variation of this is intense exercise as a way of dealing with anger. Though a little more complicated, like catharsis, exercising while angry often ends up having unintended consequences. It elevates heart rate and heavy breathing at a time when your body needs the opposite of that. Their heart is already pounding due to the anger, so exercising in that moment simply keeps the angry physiology going. In fact, exercise can even trigger angry feelings through that process of "excitation transfer" discussed before whereby the exercise-induced cardiovascular activation can increase the likelihood of responding with anger when provoked.

Crying

A very common and somewhat misunderstood response to anger is crying. I say misunderstood because many people will suggest that people cry when angry because their anger is secondary to their feelings of sadness. The person isn't really angry. They are sad, and the tears reflect that sadness. That might be true some of the time, but more often than not, those tears are just a natural, normal, and even healthy response to feeling angry.

In fact, people cry for quite a few reasons that aren't directly related to sadness. They cry when they experience physical pain, when they are scared, when they are happy, or even when they are empathizing with another person's emotions. Ultimately, tears are a communication tool. They signal to the people around you that you are in distress or feeling some intense emotions. You can think of crying as a primal help-seeking behavior that exists because it offered an evolutionary advantage to our ancestors. Those who signaled distress this way were more likely to get help and therefore more likely to survive.

Tears still work this way too. Evidence of that can be found in a 2013 study by Martijn Balsters and colleagues.[57] They showed their participants pictures of faces that were either making a sad face or a neutral face, but the researchers had added tears to half of them. The images were shown very quickly – just 50 milliseconds. The researchers then asked participants to identify (1) what emotion they expressed and (2) how much support the person needed. Participants were faster and perceived a greater need for support when the person had visible tears. Crying signals a real need for help and people pick up on that need.

Three Ways This Will Help in Dealing with Angry People

So what does this mean in the context of dealing with angry people? A few things:

No One Uses the Same Expression Style All of the Time

No one does the same thing every time they are angry. People have different anger responses that come out at different times and in different situations. Context influences anger expression considerably, in that what people do in one situation is different from what they might do in another situation (how I express my anger at my children is different from how I express it at my friends or my boss). This is, of course, expected. I'm responsible for parenting my children so if I'm frustrated with them for behaving inappropriately, I should act on that frustration in a particular way (such as, by encouraging them to act differently in the future). My relationship to my boss is very different, and so I would have different goals if I were frustrated with him. Those different goals would lead to a different expression.

People Do Have "Go-To" Expression Styles

Even though people *can* do lot of different things when they are angry (and even though their behavior will differ based on context), people do tend to gravitate toward consistent expression styles. This is particularly true with those more automatic and harder-to-control expressions (for example, tears, yelling) which happen so quickly that they are challenging to control even when the person wants to. When you have an angry person in your life, particularly someone you interact with regularly, it's best to know how they *tend* to act when they are angry. Some of the challenges that occur in these emotional moments come from a failure to realize what the person is really thinking and feeling.

Pay Attention to Where it Might Be Coming From
Finally, in dealing with angry people, you need to know where these different expression styles come from and why they might be expressing their anger that way. Their expression approach, intended or unintended, likely reflects something deeper that's going on for them. A tendency to cry might signal feelings of helplessness or powerlessness. A tendency to yell might be an attempt to control people around them through fear. A tendency to take deep breaths might signal a real attempt to calm down to work through the anger more productively. These different expressions speak to underlying issues and needs and one of the best ways to deal with angry people is to understand them and where they are coming from.

Understanding the Anger from Their Perspective

Of course, recognizing their anger is but one part of truly understanding the angry person. To really get a sense for where they are at, we need to spend some time thinking of the angry incidents from their perspective. We need to understand what provoked them, how they interpreted that provocation, and the mood they were in at the time of the provocation. We need to diagram the angry incident from their perspective. We'll cover that in the next chapter.

CHAPTER 9

STRATEGY FOUR: DIAGRAM THE ANGRY INCIDENT FROM THEIR PERSPECTIVE

They're Mad Because...

In 1991, four researchers set out to explore how well children understand emotional situations.[58] They wanted to determine if children could identify emotions when they saw them, and if they could understand the situations that led to those emotions.

The study included researchers observing preschoolers at a daycare facility. There were three groups of kids, who had been categorized based on age. The youngest group was 39 to 48 months, the middle group was 50 to 62 months, and the oldest group was 62 to 74 months. The observers waited and watched until there was an "overt happy, sad, angry, or distress expression" from one of the kids. When those expressions happened, the observer took notes on the feeling and cause, rated the intensity of the emotion, and then approached a child who was near but not involved in the emotional incident. That child was asked two questions:

- How does [target child's name] feel?*
- Why does [target child's name] feel [affect label provided by the child]?

---

* This study also revealed that boys expressed "significantly more overt anger and less overt sadness than did girls," and there was no age difference here so the gendered learning of emotional expressions we discussed in chapter 3 seems to happen before the age of three.

The researchers recorded these answers verbatim so they could be coded later and then went back to observing.* The goal here was to determine how skilled kids were at interpreting the emotions of other kids and understanding why those emotions were being felt. So the researchers were basically comparing the kids' answers with the observers' answers.

The results revealed some difference related to age and target emotion. Kids were more likely to correctly identify happiness than other emotions and they got better as they aged. In fact, the oldest group was able to correctly identify the target emotion 83 per cent of the time. Similarly, they were able to provide a general and accurate explanation of *why* the emotion was being felt at least 74 per cent of the time. Even the youngest group, made up of three- and four-year-olds, was able to accurately identify the emotion and cause about two-thirds of the time.

ANGER FACT

The vast majority of children are able to correctly identify emotions when they are displayed in real-life circumstances.

The reason I like this study is because it reveals how early kids start to understand emotional situations. There's something really fascinating about children's ability to think about emotion from another person's perspective. As infants, we were unable to even conceive of the idea that other people had thoughts and feelings. We cried in the middle of the night, completely unaware that our calls for help might be causing distress, fatigue,

---

* I am once again impressed by how meticulous researchers can be in their efforts (and once again irritated by how quick the general population is to ignore said research because of their anecdotal evidence).

or even frustration in our caregivers. We were blissfully unaware that other people might be thinking about us or even judging us. That understanding comes later… and with it a host of new emotions like shame, embarrassment, and pride. Yet, according to this research, in just a few short years we've moved from no awareness of other people's feelings to children being capable of understanding emotions nearly as well as most adults.*

There's good reason for this. Being able to understand emotional situations was crucial for our ancestors' survival. Understanding that another person or animal was angry helped them avoid conflict and stay safe in potentially hostile situations. Understanding why a person was sad helped address a loss in a way that was good for the group. Frankly, recognizing fear in someone else was adaptive simply because whatever that other person was scared of might be something you should be scared of too.

In a more modern context, understanding the what and why of emotions is a really important aspect of success in just about any interpersonal activity. A leader who understands and uses emotions effectively is better able to motivate their team. A parent who understands what their child is feeling and why they are feeling it can better attend to those emotional needs. Frankly, when I hear people complain about their co-workers, most of those complaints are not about the other person failing to do the skills of the job properly. They are complaints about the person having emotional deficits. When people describe their co-workers as odd, insensitive, disrespectful, they are describing them as lacking emotional skills.

All of this is to say that being able to understand why a person is angry from their perspective is a critical skill when it comes to dealing with angry people. It's not good enough to know that they are angry or even to have a superficial understanding

---

* Admittedly, one of the things I wonder about this study is if another interpretation could be that adults don't improve much on this skill after age six. If someone did a study that found that most kids can read as well at age six as most adults, we would be concerned about adult readers, right?

of why they are angry. Dealing with angry people is about understanding the anger from their perspective, and for that reason I encourage people to diagram the angering incident from their perspective.

Diagramming an Angry Incident

I spent much of my last book, *Why We Get Mad,* describing how to diagram an angry incident. Based on a model outlined by Dr. Jerry Deffenbacher[59], diagramming an angry incident includes identifying three interacting phenomena that lead to anger: a precipitant, the person's pre-anger state, and the appraisal process. The precipitant is the provocation. It's the thing you typically identify as having *caused* the anger. I'm mad because they didn't take the trash out like I asked. I'm angry because he took credit for my work. This precipitant can be thought of as the spark, and in that sense it does cause the anger. Imagine throwing a match onto a pile of gas-covered rags. Yes, the match started the fire, but the rags made it a whole lot worse.

Typically, when we get angry, it's because of more than just that spark. What we are doing and feeling at the time of the provocation matters too. Deffenbacher calls this the pre-anger state, and it includes our physiological and emotional state at the time we experience the precipitant. Are we tired, hungry, stressed, sad, anxious, already angry about something else, too hot or too cold, physically uncomfortable, or any other of the multitude of states that might increase our anger when we experience something aversive.

Imagine, for instance, that you get to work and open an email from a co-worker saying that they didn't finish a project that you were counting on them finishing for that day. That alone might be enough for you to get frustrated.* You were counting on

---

* Obviously, there are a bunch of contextual factors that will influence how angry you get in a situation like this: your relationship with this co-worker; their history of finishing tasks on time; how important the project was; whether you understand and trust their explanation; the consequences of their

something being done at a certain time and in a certain way, and when it wasn't done, you got angry. Your goals had been blocked, and anger is a normal and even healthy response to that sort of provocation. Now, though, imagine the same situation, but this time it happens after a terrible night's sleep or being stuck in traffic all morning on your way to work (or both). Might that provocation now feel a lot worse after a difficult morning or a sleepless night?

TIP

Understanding an angry incident from another person's perspective does not mean you tolerate abuse from that person. It is important to separate the feeling from the behavior.

One of the reasons our mood at the time of the provocation matters is because it influences the third aspect of why we get angry: the appraisal process. Appraisal refers to how we interpret the precipitant. What do we decide it means within the context of our life? Who do we think is responsible? Could it have been avoided? How bad is it? The things that happen to us aren't necessarily inherently bad or good. We decide if they are bad or good based on what they mean to us. A sunny, cloudless day might feel great to someone who is about to spend the day watching their kids play soccer. But that same day might feel frustrating to a farmer who hasn't seen rain in a while and is concerned about their crops.

having not completed it. These things all matter, but they are also up to some degree of interpretation and appraisal, and that comes later.

When people perceive situations as unfair, cruel, or interfering with their plans, they are more likely to become angry. This is where those thoughts I discussed in chapters 3, 4, and 5 come into play. People who often engage in all-or-nothing thinking, other-directed shoulds, or catastrophizing are much more likely to get angry.

How Does This Understanding Help?

So how does knowing this help you deal with an angry person? Well, an important tool for you is to be able to diagram that angry incident from their perspective. Try and understand their anger by evaluating these three elements of their angry experience. What was the precipitant? What was their mood at the time of the precipitant? And how did they interpret this precipitant as provoking to them?

When I was in college, I had a summer job on a farm with a boss who was often angry with me.* One of my responsibilities was to give tractor tours of the farm and surrounding area. That meant I was often far away from the barns and since this was an era before cell phones, I was often out of touch for long periods of time. It usually didn't matter. The tours took an hour or so, and I would be back in time for the next one.

One day, though, the group I was to give a tour to got there very late. A different boss told me to go ahead and take them, and that she would find someone else to do the next tour since I wouldn't get back in time. I went off on the tour, which took about an hour. Near the end of the tour, when we were stopped and I was describing some scenery to them, my boss came driving up on a four-wheeler looking furious.

He came over to me and said with a fake smile and pseudo-pleasant tone, "Hey Ryan, what time is it?"

I didn't have a watch, but I knew what time it was because I knew how long the tours took, so I answered him. He seemed

---

* In his defense, I was not very good at this job. During my short time there I broke multiple tractors and had a very unfortunate incident where I covered the kitchen, including one of the owners, with about six gallons of unfiltered apple cider.

surprised that I was correct, so he followed up, this time with more anger in his voice, "No. Look at your fucking watch and tell me what time it is."

"You know I don't have a watch, but I know what ti—"

"That's right. You don't have a fucking watch," he said, cutting me off, "and so you don't know that you're late for your next tour. You need to get a fucking watch."

"I know what time it is," I responded. "They got here late, and I was told to take them anyway. Someone else was going to cover the next tour."

He was dumbstruck. He was obviously unaware of this information, and didn't have anything to say in response. This was all happening in front of the tour, by the way, which added a layer of weirdness and discomfort to the entire situation. There was a long, awkward pause, and then he said, "Well I obviously didn't know that. Thanks for letting me know. I'm going to get back and make sure that next tour is taken care of."

Then he drove off on the four-wheeler, leaving me to deal with the embarrassment and unease of everyone who had witnessed the odd exchange. But let's take a moment to break this situation down. I'll be clear at the outset that I think he behaved very badly. He reacted without knowing the full situation, treated me unnecessarily cruelly, and did so in a way that was embarrassing to him, me, and the people on the tour. Even if I was truly in error in this situation, giving him a fair reason to be angry with me, there were a lot of better and more productive ways to handle it.

Considering it from His Perspective

This is how to diagram the incident into three stages:

The Precipitant

The precipitant is simple (it usually is). I wasn't where he thought I was supposed to be and there was no one to give the next tour. This falls solidly in the goal-blocking category of provocations. He wanted his guests to have a positive experience and starting a tour late because there was no one to run it was interfering with that goal.

The Pre-Anger State

His pre-anger state is a little harder to judge, but I'll take a guess that he was stressed and a little anxious. This was both an active farm and a popular spot for families to visit on weekends, especially at that time of year. It got exceedingly busy and everyone had multiple jobs to do at a given time. That high level of stress likely put him on edge. He and the others on the farm also worked really long days on the weekends during the busy season, starting very early in the morning to set up before they opened and continuing well into the evening after they closed. I imagine he was fairly exhausted as well.

The Appraisal

What makes this situation most interesting, though, is the appraisal. It's valuable to imagine how he thought about this situation and the people involved. Let's think about the situation itself separate from his thoughts about me. From his perspective, there was a tour I was supposed to lead and I wasn't there to lead it. This immediately kicked off thoughts related to other-directed shoulds:

- "Ryan should have been here."
- "This is his job."
- "What's he even doing right now?"

He was also likely fixating on the consequences of there not being a tour guide, and maybe even catastrophizing those consequences (exaggerating how negative this situation really was).

- "We're going to have to refund this group's money."
- "This is really embarrassing."
- "I'm so busy and now I'm going to have to give this tour."

This appraisal is already likely to lead to anger. Anyone who experiences a situation like this and appraises it in this way is likely to get angry. But it's made even worse when you factor in his perceptions of me. I was not very good at this job. I was a responsible employee in most ways – I got to work on time, did what was asked of me, worked well with our customers, but I just didn't have many of the skills or background knowledge to be good at this job. I had almost no experience with tractors or engines before working there, and much of my day was spent driving them. Most of their tractors were pretty old and in disrepair too, so they would break down in various ways and I never knew what to do in those moments (nor could I anticipate the problems the way others could).

What this meant for my boss is that I was constantly involved in problems (from his perspective, *causing* those problems). So when I wasn't there to give the tour, he jumped to the conclusion that I was to blame. As we discussed earlier, this sort of misattribution of causation can often exacerbate our anger. To take it a step further, he went on to assume the cause of my not being there for the tour – that I didn't have a watch and didn't know what time it was.* In the end, he was wrong on both counts. I wasn't to blame and I did know what time it was, but from his perspective these were the factors that had caused this situation (a situation he was defining as relatively catastrophic).

Plus, there was some inflammatory labeling of me that likely took hold from him, as he was thinking I was "irresponsible," "stupid," or far worse. These labels we give people in those angering moments are important because once we label people, we start thinking of them in those ways. They become a lens through which we view the person. It feeds into that perception problem because he starts thinking of me as a stupid and

---

* For reasons I can't fully explain, it really bothered him that I didn't own a watch. I suspect it was an unwritten rule he had for how responsible people *should* behave ("responsible people have watches"). It's sort of funny because I always knew what time it was and I wasn't chronically late by any means (there were plenty of clocks around), but he really wanted me to own a watch anyway.

irresponsible employee and forgets the parts of the job I'm good at or the ways I'm responsible.

So, putting this all together, we have an exhausted and stressed person (pre-anger state) encountering a situation where their goals are blocked (precipitant) in a way they find to be both embarrassing and catastrophic (appraisal). The situation was caused by an irresponsible employee (appraisal). He became quite enraged over this (feeling state), and expressed it by finding me and yelling at me (expression).

Using this Information to De-Escalate

So what does this diagram get me as the victim of the angry outburst? Two things:

How to Intervene

First, it helps tell me where to intervene in the moment. In this case, the anger was stemming from a few particular sources:

- Stress and exhaustion
- Misinformation about what happened
- Perceptions of me as irresponsible

As his employee, it's not really my place to try and deal with the stress and exhaustion. Plus, that's a difficult task in a situation like this. No one likes being told to relax or to take a break (especially by an employee). I can, however, work to address the misinformation. Ultimately, in this case the de-escalation was simply to clarify that misinformation.

Understanding Patterns

Second, over time, diagramming angry incidents like this can give you a sense for patterns when you regularly interact with an angry person. In this case, his anger at me often stemmed from his perceptions of me as irresponsible and incompetent. I can take steps to address those perceptions either through direct conversation ("I get the sense you think I'm irresponsible. Can we talk about what I can do to change that?") or through more indirect approaches (I can find ways to demonstrate my responsibilities/competence to him). Similarly, when you know enough about a person to understand their triggers (both provocations and mood states), you're better able to work through those things effectively. You can avoid situations you know will set them off. You can recognize when they are in a mood that is likely to lead to anger before the anger happens, and you can take some steps to preempt the anger.

TIP

Pay attention to patterns in how and why a person gets angry. Being able to identify those patterns allows you to better work through potential angry incidents in the future.

When the Anger is Warranted

Of course, there is one more reason why we might want to think about the anger from the other person's perspective. In the case above, I wasn't at fault. I didn't do anything wrong (this time) and my boss's anger at me was misdirected. But that isn't always the case. Sometimes we really are at fault for something and the other person's anger at us – not necessarily their treatment of us, but their anger at us – is justified. How can we deal with angry people when the anger is warranted? We come on to this in the next chapter.

CHAPTER 10

STRATEGY FIVE: ASK WHETHER THE ANGER IS JUSTIFIED

When What Should Be an Easy Thing is Actually a Hard Thing

I want you to take a moment to imagine a situation when someone is angry with you, and it's perfectly clear that you did something wrong to earn that anger. Maybe it was unintentional. Maybe it was minor. Maybe their anger is far greater than it *should* be given what you did, but it is still very evident that their anger is justified. You made a mistake and they got mad over that mistake. Now it's time to try and resolve the situation if you can.

Recognizing you did something wrong and working to address it should be an easy thing to do. What I mean is that the actual steps involved here are pretty simple. You look at the situation, diagramming it the way I described in the previous chapter if you need to. You identify your role in the situation, determine where you made mistakes, admit it, and work to identify a resolution. On their own, void of any emotion, those steps are simple. So, why isn't this as easy as it should be? One reason... defensiveness.

How Do You Know Whether Their Anger is Justified?

Before we get to defensiveness, let's talk about how you know whether their anger is justified. Because even when you separate out the defensiveness, determining whether they are right to be angry can be tricky. There is no litmus test for this sort of thing and such a determination always depends on context. What did you do, what prompted it, how might they have interpreted it, and so on. Here are a couple of suggestions, though, to guide your thinking:

Don't Let Their Anger Make the Decision for You

Sometimes, we unintentionally let another person's emotions dictate our own feelings of culpability or guilt. We think that because the other person is mad at us, we must have done something wrong. Try to avoid thinking and feeling that way. Other people's anger is not necessarily an indicator of our mistake. It might mean that we have made an error, but there are plenty of times when other people are simply wrong and their feelings toward us are not justified. They may have misinterpreted the situation or they may be overreacting. Frankly, they may be using their anger as a weapon and gaslighting you. You need to separate their reaction to what you did from what you actually did.

Evaluate What You Did and the Impact on Them and Not *Why* You Did It

You will sometimes hear people say, "I realize it came across as mean, but I was just trying to…" and then they fill in that blank with a justification of whatever they did. Obviously, for our own emotional wellbeing, growth, and development, that justification matters. It's good for us to unpack the various factors that influence why we do the things we do. But from the perspective of the other person who is mad at us, what we were *trying* to do or *why* we did it doesn't really matter that much. What matters most is what we did and the impact it had on them.

What we really need to ask ourselves is "Did I treat them poorly or unfairly?" or "Did I somehow unreasonably block their goals?" Regardless of what motivated it, did my actions harm them by making them feel badly, taking away an opportunity, or slowing them down. If so, their anger is justified.

Defensiveness

Defensiveness is an emotional response to being (or believing you are being) criticized or attacked. You get defensive when you think you are being accused of having done something wrong. Like any emotion, it includes thoughts, physiological arousals, and behaviors. For instance, imagine your partner gets angry with you for not cleaning up a mess you made. In your heart, you know you made a mistake. You were going to clean it up, but you just forgot. Instead of just saying, "I'm sorry, I'll clean it up as soon as I can," you get defensive about it. You might:

- Think something like "They make messes and forget to clean up all the time, so why am I getting criticized?" (thoughts).
- Feel a slight increase in heart rate or muscle tension, consistent with anxiety, shame, or nervousness (physiological arousal).
- Become sarcastic and accusatory ("Oh, because *you've* never forgotten to clean up before") or even deny the mistake* (behavior).

Also like any other emotion, defensiveness is more likely to occur under particular circumstances. In fact, you could diagram your or someone else's defensiveness in a way that is similar to how you diagram anger, by identifying the stimulus that led to it (being criticized), the pre-defensiveness state (the mood you were in at the time of the criticism), and your appraisal of the stimulus ("I shouldn't have to hear this," "Who are they to criticize me?").

---

* For whatever reason, I have a hard time admitting in the moment that I forgot to turn off a light. I know I have a bad habit of leaving lights on, but when my wife tells me I left one on, I try desperately to find ways to deny it. I will do all sorts of cognitive gymnastics to blame it on someone else. As I write this, unencumbered by defensiveness because I'm not in the moment, I can tell you that it's a totally and completely unreasonable feeling to have and position to take. In that moment, though, I find all sorts of ways to deflect. Honestly, if I could reasonably blame it on the dog, I would.

What makes defensiveness particularly concerning is that taking feedback is really important for growth and improvement. Regardless of role or activity (employee, spouse, boss, student, friend, teammate, performer), you need to be open to criticism to improve. It's why just about every graduate school or job reference form I've ever filled out asks if the person is receptive to feedback.

TIP

Take time to think about what you want your core values to be. Are you kind? Are you honest? Do you want to continue to learn and grow? An awareness of your values will influence how you act when confronted.

Why do people get defensive in response to another person's anger at them? Why is it so hard for people to admit they made a mistake and work to resolve it? It is a particularly strange phenomenon when you consider that many people get especially frustrated when other people don't admit and apologize for their mistakes. "I just wish they would admit what they did was wrong and apologize" is a very common refrain when it comes to conflict. So, there's this disconnect between what many people want from others and what they are willing to do themselves. Why?

Threats to Our Self-Identity

Like most emotional experiences, defensiveness is about self-protection. Being accused of an error is perceived as a threat to our wellbeing or our identity, and we react with distress. That distress motivates us to seek some sort of comfort and resolution. If we were able to think rationally in that moment, the comfort and resolution would come from owning the mistake and addressing it. But when we can't think rationally, we seek resolution by denying the mistake or trying to refocus the conflict on the other person. "I'm sorry I forgot to do the dishes" turns into "Yeah, well you never put the laundry away like you're supposed to!"

ANGER FACT

Defensiveness is a natural emotional reaction to having identity threatened. It's protective in the same way other emotions are protective, but it can still interfere with progress.

It's even more of a threat when the error is inconsistent with your self-identity. If someone accused me being a bad fisherman, I wouldn't care. I don't identify as being good at this activity so being told I'm bad at it doesn't feel like a threat to my identity. If, though, someone accused me of being, or implied I was, a bad teacher, parent, or spouse, I would care. I want to be, and work really hard to be, good at those things, so the implication that I'm not doing them well is hurtful to me. When someone notices I made an error – no matter how small – that suggests I'm not doing a good job in one of these roles, it serves as a threat to an important part of my self-identity, and it hurts.

It may not be as obvious as the examples here. Our identity can be broad and diffuse and challenged in all sorts of vague and unexpected ways. A great basketball player may feel attacked when challenged about some other sport simply because they identify as an athlete. The challenge feels like an attack on their natural athletic ability. A person who values kindness may feel threatened when told they came across as rude or impolite during an interaction. They see the feedback as a threat to their identity as a kind and considerate person.*

There are a number of personal characteristics that might make you more likely to become defensive when someone is angry with you. You might be insecure or lack confidence. You might be anxious or have difficulty asserting yourself when challenged. You might have a history of trauma or abuse that makes these situations more emotionally taxing for you. You may have had defensiveness modeled for you in the same way other emotional expressions are modeled and it became a learned behavior. Just like any emotional experience, the roots of defensiveness can be complicated and extend beyond the specific thing that provoked it.

Of course, where the feedback is coming from matters too, and so does the environment in which you get the feedback. Take, for instance, a 2019 study by Levi Adelman and Nilanjana Dasgupta that explored how people react to "ingroup criticism."[60] Ingroup criticism is negative feedback that comes from inside. It's when a teammate, spouse, or colleague tells you that you need to do something differently. In this paper, which includes three separate studies, the authors explored how people took in criticism under different sets of circumstances. Participants were assigned to a "threat" or a "no-threat" group. The "threat" group read an article about how the economy was stagnating and how this could lead to lower wages and a worse quality of life. Within those two groups, participants also read an article about how the stagnating economy was the result of American's poor work ethic (so the participants, who were all Americans, are essentially being blamed for the poor economic conditions). This second article is written by an economist and expert on the American economy, but that expert's nationality is manipulated

---

* This explains the leaving the lights on example earlier. I like to think of myself as a responsible person who cares about the environment. As minor as it is, this habit of leaving lights on is really inconsistent with the person I want to be, so I get defensive about the fact that I can't seem to fix it.

to add another variable to the study. They are either American (ingroup) or South Korean (outgroup).

What they found was that when there was no threat (when participants hadn't read the article about how they would likely soon be experiencing a worse quality of life and lower wages), they were more receptive to ingroup feedback than outgroup feedback. In other words, they got more defensive when the criticism came from a South Korean. But, when they felt under threat, that receptiveness to ingroup criticism declined. When participants feared for their own economic wellbeing, there was no difference. They got defensive regardless. This speaks to the idea that at its core, defensiveness is about protection from what we perceive to be a threat to our emotional or general wellbeing.

How to Know Whether You're Being Defensive and What to Do About It

Like any emotional experience, it can be difficult to realize in the moment when you are being defensive. By definition, you aren't necessarily thinking clearly and are not able to adequately assess your own feelings, thoughts, and behaviors. So, how can you catch yourself when defensiveness kicks in?

First, you might catch yourself trying to refocus the conversation onto the actions of the other person. This might include focusing on what they did that *made you* do what you did. It also might include focusing on how they have wronged you or engaged in similar behavior as you in the past. Both of these might reflect an attempt to ignore your role in the offense in favor of the other person's role.

Second, you might find that you aren't really listening to the person. You may be thinking about what you want to say next instead of listening to what they are saying to you. If it's an email or a text, you may delay reading it or even stop reading midway through. Finally, you might find yourself using some "yeah, but" logic in how you respond by saying things like, "I know I shouldn't have done that, but…" or "I hear what you're saying, but…." Often, that sort of logic might illustrate a tendency to try and deflect.

TIP

Pay attention to when you are trying to refocus away from what you did to what the other person did. That is often a pretty good indicator of defensiveness.

Obviously, chronic defensiveness can bring with it some significant consequences; some to you and some to those around you. For you, it can eventually lead to feelings of guilt and shame. In the moment, deflecting can help you feel better about an emotional situation, but the long-term impact might be that you end up feeling guilty, embarrassed, or even sad about how you acted. It can also lead to significant relationship problems. Interpersonal situations become more hostile and emotional than they otherwise would have. People start to see you as unreasonable or someone they can't trust. Potentially the biggest problem, though, is that it prevents you from solving problems effectively and coming to a reasonable resolution.

If defensiveness is preventing you from effectively working through emotional situations, here are some strategies to overcome it. Some of these require effort in the moment but others are things you can work on right now.

Explore Your Identity

If defensiveness emerges when your identity is challenged, then it makes sense to spend some time exploring your identity. When are the times when you feel especially defensive and what aspects of your identity are challenged in those moments? To take it a step further, are there ways you can think about your identity differently that might lead to less defensiveness? For instance, can you shift from "I need to be right" to "I like to learn things." Such a shift means that when you get something wrong, you see it as an opportunity for growth instead of a challenge to your intellect.

In that above paper by Adelman and Dasgupta, there was a particularly fascinating outcome that could shed some additional light on how to address defensiveness as it relates to your identity. In one of the studies they ran, they tried an intervention to decrease defensiveness where they reminded people of a "core national value." They had half of the participants read a statement about the value of free speech before participating in the study (the same procedure as above). They found that this framing device increased participants' receptiveness to the criticism regardless of the presence of a threat or the source of the criticism. Reminding people of a relevant core value decreased their likelihood of defensiveness.

So, in these moments of defensiveness, take time to remind yourself of your core values that relate to the situation. When you've done something wrong and a person is mad at you, take time to remind yourself who you are and what you care about. Similar to the study above, frame the experience around your values.

Anticipate Moments of Defensiveness

You may be able to predict some moments when you will feel defensive. Perhaps there are particular people (such as a boss, a parent) who tend to put you on edge or perhaps there are particular situations (a type of work meeting, a holiday gathering) that tend to bring it out of you. Once you have a sense for when these moments are coming, you can prepare for them. You can make some decisions about how you want to handle it and what you want to say *before* you find yourself overcome by the emotion.

Find (or Create) a Pause (Again)

In chapter 7, I wrote about how to stay calm in these emotional situations. All of those same suggestions remain relevant here. Deep breathing, relaxation, and grounding are all valuable ways to keep from reacting in a way you'll regret. But before you can do any of that, you need to find a way to pause in the moment. It's an important step in reclaiming focus to find that pause button as soon as you recognize the escalation.

What They Did vs. What They Feel

It's important to always remember that what a person feels is different but related to what they did with that feeling. A person can be angry with you, and that anger might be entirely valid, but that doesn't mean they can treat you in whatever way they please. Justified anger doesn't make it ok for a person to yell at you or say cruel and hurtful things to you. Remembering this is important for two reasons.

First, it is very easy, especially when feeling defensive, to focus on how they are behaving and ignore the underlying feelings. Their behavior becomes a reason to ignore their anger, which may be justified and rooted in a very real injustice that you are responsible for.* While you do not need to subject yourself to cruel treatment, trying to separate what they did from how they feel might allow you to more effectively right a wrong. If you are able to say to yourself, "Their anger is fair even thought their behavior is not," you can move forward to try and resolve both issues by conveying that (1) you made a mistake you wish to resolve and (2) you expect better treatment moving forward.

Second, the opposite of this last point is also true. While you should not discount their feelings because you don't approve of

---

* I have noticed it is sometimes an intentional strategy for people to focus on the behaviors of angry people in order to minimize the justified anger behind those feelings. Protesters, for instance, are often maligned for their tactics as a way to diminish their concerns. You hear it in the expressions of journalists and politicians who say things like, "I understand their concerns, but I wish they would voice those concerns in a different way."

or appreciate their behaviors, you should not let their justified feelings serve as an excuse for them to treat you poorly. I've heard people say, for instance, things like, "I deserved that after what I did to them" as a way of explaining away cruelty. It is totally reasonable to convey to someone that while you recognize the harm you may have caused them and that they should be angry, you are unwilling to tolerate their cruelty. As is always the case, you can walk away from toxic people and toxic situations in your life.

How to Apologize

So what can you do in those moments when you've decided their anger is justified and that you have done something wrong you wish to make up for. We can't always right the wrongs we've caused, but we can take steps to do what is possible. Those steps will likely start with an apology.

Even once you've removed defensiveness from the equation, apologizing can be difficult for people. It's a really important thing to do, though, as it can help repair the damaged relationship and open the door to a meaningful resolution regarding the specific situation where you are in error. There is also the added benefit that it can help you experience less guilt over the mistake because you're taking steps to address it. With all that in mind, here are three important steps to apologizing:

First, take responsibility for what you did and make sure that is reflected in the language you use as you apologize. Saying "I'm sorry, but…" or "I'm sorry if…" doesn't necessarily reflect a true and sincere apology. But saying, "I'm sorry I [hurt your feelings/didn't finish that report/forgot to call you]" does acknowledge that you made a mistake and you're taking responsibility for it.

Second, make sure they know you feel remorse or sadness over what you did. Again, this can be reflected in the language you use when you apologize by saying things like, "I really regret having done this" or "I feel sad for having made you feel this way."

Third, make an attempt, or at least offer, to fix the parts you are able to fix. If you didn't get something done at work they are counting on, help problem-solve with them to minimize the impact. If you broke their trust, tell them you will work to avoid doing that in the future.

Of course, some of these situations will take time to resolve and it's unreasonable and unfair to expect people to suddenly become less angry simply because you apologized. Forgiveness can take time and energy and even the most deep and sincere apology doesn't undo the potential damage.

Not Every Angry Person Lets You Know It

Of course, not every angry person wants to communicate. As you know already, anger can be expressed in a lot of different ways and sometimes angry people shut down and go silent. How do you deal with an angry person who simply won't communicate with you? What do you do if they won't even admit to you that they are mad? We'll take that on in the next chapter.

CHAPTER 11

STRATEGY SIX: FIND WAYS TO REACH THOSE WHO REFUSE TO COMMUNICATE

Cutting Off Contact

A client, Anne, once came to talk to me because she had alienated a friend and didn't know what to do about it. It had started over something small, but had escalated into a bigger fight, and Anne had hurt her friend's feelings. Her friend then completely disconnected from her. She stopped responding to calls and texts (this was in the era before social media, but I suspect she would have unfriended her on Facebook as well), and when they bumped into each other on her college campus, the friend just walked past her without saying anything or making eye contact.

Anne was devastated. She missed her friend and felt bad about what she had done to alienate her. What made things more complicated for her, though, was that she didn't actually think she was fully responsible. She told me that they had both gone too far with the argument, that they both had said hurtful things to one another, and that they both had good reasons to be angry. Anne didn't feel it was entirely her responsibility to try and save their friendship, but she also knew her friend wasn't going to put forward any effort. This last piece made her feel even worse.

The situation between Anne and her friend is a relationship problem, obviously, but it's also an anger problem. At the core, we have two people who are angry at one another and one of them is expressing that anger by cutting off contact. Anne interpreted that shutting down as a lack of interest in continuing the friendship, and that may have been true, but it also might not have been true.

TIP

When someone cuts off contact with you because they are angry with you, spend some time considering what's driving it. Are they hurt, uncomfortable with conflict, trying to manipulate you? Do they want to end the relationship, or something else? The answer to these questions provides a window into how you might move forward with them.

"It's Not My Job to Manage Their Emotions"

As I was writing this chapter, I became curious as to how people would handle this type of situation. So I asked on social media for people to tell me what they would do. I posted a TikTok video and it got 200 responses in just a few hours. The responses varied quite a bit with people saying things like:

- "Depends… but if it's someone I care about, I would reach out via text and ask them what's going on and what I can do to help fix it."
- "I'd take it as a sign they don't want to talk about it. I'd respect their choice not to talk, and give them space. They'll talk when they want to."
- "It's their responsibility to communicate their needs/ grievances. We can't force them to step up to the plate."
- "I'd ask them about it once and I'd leave a low-pressure open-ended, *If you ever want to talk about this, the door is open*, and then just leave them alone."

- "I'd ignore it. I'd just act like I don't realize. It'll wear them down and they'll either tell me or poof, gone. Either way it's their choice. It has to be."

Overall, the general sense was somewhere between *I'll reach out once and let them know I'm here* and *I'll do nothing. It's their problem. It's not my job to manage their emotions.*

A few people pointed out something really important about situations like these, though, and it's that we don't actually know why Anne's friend cut off contact. A lot of the responders assumed it was because she didn't want the relationship anymore. Others assumed it was because she was immature, manipulative, or even wanted Anne to beg for her friendship. Those are all possible, but there might be other reasons too. Remember, anger can be expressed in a lot of different ways, and a person's expression style might not be intentional or planned. It may simply be what they are comfortable with or what they learned was the best way to express.

What's Driving It?

It doesn't have to be as dramatic as Anne's situation above. Sometimes it is. Sometimes the person just flat-out avoids you. They don't respond to calls, emails, and texts, and they ignore you when you see them in person. Alternatively, maybe they have just pulled back on their involvement with you, but not cut you off completely. They might still respond to you, but it's become increasingly impersonal and your interactions are largely superficial compared to how they once were. Their anger toward you has had long-term negative effects that derailed the relationship.

But the cause might not be what you think (at least, it might be more complicated than seems obvious at first). Yes, it started with a disagreement that led to anger, but it doesn't necessarily follow that the reason they have cut off contact is just that anger. When people stop communicating the way Anne's friend did, it might be because they are mad at you, or it might be something else. Quick caveat, though, that almost all of the research on this topic has looked at "ghosting" * in romantic relationships – where one partner abruptly disappears instead of ending the relationship – so we need to extrapolate from that to other types of relationships. Here are a few different possible explanations.

Embarrassment

Sometimes people shut down like this out of embarrassment over the way they acted during the argument. They might not realize it or even do it intentionally, but contacting the person they had the fight with means facing the situation again in a way that makes them uncomfortable. They are ashamed and self-conscious and avoidance is the path of least discomfort. By cutting off contact with you, they don't have to revisit what they said or did.

Sadness, Hurt, or Depression

Sometimes, the lack of contact is motivated by deep feelings of sadness or even depression. Their initial anger has given way to now feeling hurt by something you did or said. It might not even be that you did or said anything specific, but simply the fact that you disagreed (or their interpretation of what that disagreement means) has led to some emotional pain for them. Contacting you would exacerbate that hurt so they are avoiding it.

Discomfort with Conflict

Conflict is difficult and it makes some people very uncomfortable and even anxious. When people shut down like this or avoid contact with you, it might simply be because they are trying

---

* I will admit to being pleasantly surprised by the amount of research that's been done on "ghosting." There's about 20 research articles in the past decade, which is a good amount considering it's a relatively new topic. I was not disappointed with the titles either which ranged from the punny (*When your boo becomes a ghost*) to the excessively jargony (*Disappearing in the age of hypervisibility: Definition, context, and perceived psychological consequences of social media ghosting*).

to avoid dealing with something that's very hard for them. Avoidance is a natural and common reaction to fear and anxiety so the distress they feel over the conflict encourages them to avoid the relationship.

Passive-Aggressive Manipulation

Shutting down like this might be motivated by a passive-aggressive attempt to hurt the person they are in conflict with. They know that cutting off contact with the person will hurt them and that is their intent. It might even be a way of gaining an upper-hand in the relationship, by sending the message that they don't need the relationship. They want the person to apologize and even beg for forgiveness.

A Genuine Desire to End the Relationship

It's quite possible that cutting off contact reflects a genuine desire to end the relationship. This could be motivated by a whole host of feelings, including the sadness, hurt, embarrassment, or discomfort with conflict mentioned here. Regardless, they might simply be done with the friendship and want to move on. This might not be the most mature way to handle things, but it happens often.*

Attempting to Reconnect

So what do you do in a situation like this? How can you deal effectively with a person who is (likely) angry with you and has cut off all contact?

---

* The internet is of two minds on this topic. On the one hand, "ghosting" appears very common and some see it as a reasonable way to end relationships, particularly if those relationships were unhealthy. At the same time, essays on how to deal with ghosting are actively hostile to the "ghosts," routinely describing them as immature or even too unskilled to communicate directly. The ghosts themselves were not available to respond.

Make Sure You Know the Reason Why They Cut Off Contact

It's important to understand these different explanations because they likely require different solutions. A person who has cut off contact because they are embarrassed by something they did or said might require a different response from you than a person who is quite angry with you but is avoiding conflict. Both might require gentleness from you, but the later might also need to be given some permission and coaxing to say what they want to say.

Frankly, knowing the source might actually lead you to not want to do anything at all about it. If you realize, for instance, that the person is being manipulative or passive-aggressive, you may decide that this is not a relationship you want to invest energy in. Even the person who is avoiding conflict might not be someone you want to do anything about. You may decide, as was said to me by many people on social media, that it isn't your responsibility to manage the emotions of others. Depending on the nature of the relationship and what this person means to you, that might be a reasonable option.

Consider What You're Willing to Do for This Relationship

By definition, repairing a relationship where someone is refusing to communicate with you requires effort on your part. At a minimum, it will require that you break the silence by reaching out, but it might require even more than that. Preserving the relationship could mean you need to apologize for something you did (maybe even something you don't feel completely responsible for). It might mean you need to swallow some of your feelings to protect the other person's feelings. You need to decide what this relationship means to you and what you are willing to do to preserve it.

There are a lot of things to factor into that decision. Who the person is in your life (such as friend, co-worker, family), the relationships they have with other people in your life, the power they might have over you, your feelings, and so on. These added dynamics will play into the situation in a significant way. What you choose to do to preserve the relationship will necessarily depend on who they are and what they mean to your life.

Decide What is Most Important

In chapter 6, I wrote about the importance of having a goal in mind when interacting with angry people. That continues to be true in these situations. If you are going to reach out to someone who is angry with you and has cut off contact, what is your goal and how can you obtain that goal? Do you want to preserve the relationship? Do you want to make sure they understand your position on whatever the dispute was about? Do you want to get the last word in and say goodbye? Each of these goals likely requires a different approach. To preserve the relationship, you might need to stop yourself from saying some things you really want to say. To make sure they understand your position, you'll need to be honest in ways you and they might not be comfortable with. Be thoughtful about your goal and how to get there but also be flexible about what they might want.

Put the Ball in Their Court

If and when you decide to reach out, do so via a channel that will work best for both of you. For instance, Ephraim, who I described in chapter 5, really valued texting for difficult conversations. He said he appreciated the time to think and compose his thoughts. That might be something you or the person you are reaching out to could value (especially important considering that if they've cut off contact, they might not answer the phone if you call). Regardless of how you reach out, let them know how you're feeling in a direct but non-hostile way, and empower them to take the next step (for instance, "I think you must be angry with me and I would like to talk about it with you. Please let me know when you're ready.").

> **TIP**
>
> Scheduling a time to talk in person or on the phone can be helpful. It provides an opportunity to plan and prepare psychologically for the discussion.

If/When They Respond, Be Open to Feedback, and Listen

If you do get the opportunity to communicate with them in person or via text/email, make sure to be flexible and open to feedback. Listen to their position with an open mind. As was discussed in chapter 10, it is natural and normal to get defensive in moments like these. You may feel attacked in response to something they say and it's best to prepare for that possible feeling in advance. Go into the interaction with a plan for what you want to communicate, consistent with what you have already decided is most important, but be prepared for the possibility of things going a different direction than you expected. Solving whatever problem may have led to this situation will necessarily be a joint effort, so you'll need to be prepared to work together on identifying solutions.

Know When to Give Up

You may not want to hear this, but there may come a point where you just need to give up. Remember that one of the reasons why they may have cut off contact is because of a genuine desire to end the relationship. If that's the case, it may be impossible for you to do anything to change their mind. In fact, continuing to try and rebuild the relationship after they have made it clear they don't want to is disrespectful to them. Listening to them means respecting their wishes and backing away when that is what they want.

Alternatively, you may decide through this process that you no longer want to have a relationship with this person. You may decide the relationship is too much work or simply not good for you anymore. You may start to see unexpected emotional consequences of being in a relationship with them that don't seem worth it when you consider the big picture. That is ok too.

Take Care of Yourself

It is undeniable that this sort of interaction will take an emotional toll on you. If you do have the conversation, it can be emotionally draining and uncomfortable. Be aware of the fact that you might need a break or that you might even need to call it quits for the day in order to get some rest and some distance from the situation. Using some of the strategies to stay calm, discussed in chapter 7, might be really important here.

At the same time, if the person doesn't respond and you never have the conversation, it can be emotionally draining and painful in a different way. Them making the decision that they no longer want you in their life, regardless of what led to them making that decision, will likely be hurtful and distressing. You might blame yourself and feel ashamed and responsible for the problem. It's important to do what you can to take care of yourself, stay resilient, and learn from the experience.

ANGER FACT

A damaged relationship is one of the most common consequences of maladaptive anger, with most Anger Project survey respondents saying they have harmed at least one relationship in the past month because of their anger.[61]

The Hostility of the Internet

The outcome for Anne was not such a pleasant one. Anne reached out to her friend via email, asking for an opportunity to talk about what had happened and even issuing an apology for her part of it. What she got back from her friend was an exceedingly hostile response, making it clear – maybe even a little too clear – that she did not wish to be friends anymore. Anne was hurt and therapy quickly shifted from "How can I repair this friendship?" to "How can I get over this loss?"

It does open up a really interesting question, though, about how to deal with an angry email. Or, more broadly, how do we deal with various forms of "e-anger" (social media, texting, dating apps, and so on)? Much of the anger we experience isn't face to face, but screen to screen. What are some effective strategies for navigating the hostility of the internet? The next chapter is all about that.

CHAPTER 12

STRATEGY SEVEN: STEP AWAY FROM ONLINE RAGE

The "Non-Ignorable Role" of Anger Online

In 2014 Rui Fan and colleagues set out to discover the online contagiousness of particular emotions.[62] They wanted to know which emotions spread most quickly across social media. Using Weibo, a Chinese platform they described as similar to Twitter, they captured approximately 70 million posts from 278,654 users. They coded the emotionality of these posts (based on emoticon usage, caps, and other factors) into four categories: disgust, sadness, joy, and anger. They then looked to see which posts were most likely to be liked or shared by others.

What they found was fascinating, though, not necessarily surprising to anyone who has spent considerable time online over the past decade. People didn't typically share posts associated with disgust or sadness, at least not compared with their sharing of joyful or angry posts. They did share joyful posts, when they were connected to the person who shared the original post. They shared angry posts, though, whether they were connected to the person or not. In other words, people joined in the joy of others when they knew them, but joined in the anger whether they knew them or not. This led the authors to write "we conjecture that anger plays a non-ignorable role in massive propagations of the negative news about the society."*

---

* This quote is somewhat jaw-dropping when you consider what's happened since it was written in 2014 and how public anger has informed those events. Both the 2016 and 2020 US elections were driven largely by anger, much of it propagated by social media.

How Online Emotions Are Similar/Different

What the study above really shows is something most of you have already noticed, that anger is omnipresent online. You likely encounter angry people in your online interactions a couple of times a week to a couple of times per day. Maybe they are people you know and are interacting with via email, text, or Messenger, or maybe they are strangers you encounter on social media and will never connect with again. What's fascinating, though, is that even though the consequences of an online argument with a stranger may be different than such an argument with a friend, the causes of such anger are very similar.

There are relatively simple explanations for why we encounter angry people online as often as we do, and it's because social media and electronic forms of communication like email and texting have changed how we experience and express our emotions in significant ways. It's provided new venues to express our emotions, given us additional stimuli to respond to, and even changed how we interpret those stimuli.

More Opportunities to Feel

Every morning I get up and make myself some coffee. While it's brewing, I scroll through Facebook or Twitter or some other social-media platform, catching up on what's happened in the nine or ten hours since I last checked. In doing so, I'm exposed to all sorts of stimuli to respond to emotionally. I may feel joy learning that an old friend is getting married, sadness to see someone I care about has gotten sick, or anger over political news shared by a co-worker. These are opportunities to feel things that I didn't have in the same way 15 years ago. I might never have learned that that old friend was getting married because we had lost contact. I get to feel happy for them now in a way I wouldn't have prior to social media.

As a consequence of this, we have all sorts of minor and major emotional experiences throughout our day (depending on how often we scroll through our various social-media feeds). But it's not just social media. We are connected to news outlets now in ways we never were before. A couple of decades ago, most people checked the news just a few times a day, maybe through the newspaper or through a nightly news program on TV. Now, though, news comes through immediately via app or email alerts. Even if you choose to avoid that sort of technology, the omnipresence of news media means we undoubtedly hear about it more often via those friends, co-workers, and family who are heavily connected. Like social media, this ends up impacting our emotional life because this added news content is not emotionally neutral.[63*] It's yet another opportunity to feel.

New Venues and New Languages

Electronic forms of communication like texting, email, and social media have given people another place and even another language to express their feelings. When people are angry at someone, they can communicate that anger in ways that were never possible before. They can fire off an angry email to the person that wronged them, tweet directly at the company they are angry at, or just post on Facebook for their friends to see. This is a fundamentally different way to express anger, which has a significant impact on you and the world around you. When you add that some of these venues are anonymous or at least feel anonymous to the user, they quickly become a place for rage to spread.

It's not just the change of venue for angry expressions that is offered by the internet – technology has given us new languages to express anger. What might have started with rudimentary emoticons such as :-) has evolved into much more complicated but fascinating expressions. Emojis, hashtags, memes, and GIFs are all used to share anger in humorous and not humorous ways. Meanwhile, YouTube, TikTok, Instagram, and other video/photo-sharing sites are full of videos of people ranting

---

* Far from it. According to the 2012 study by Drs. Jonah Berger and Katherine Milkman, news content that evokes high-arousal emotions, particularly anger or fear, are more likely to go viral. So the material that makes its way to you is likely to evoke those feelings.

about things that make them mad. The ability to easily make and edit a video to express anger is wildly different from what people used to do when angry. Plus, social media has opened the door to more passive-aggressive expressions of anger. Angry people use social media to spread rumors or even to shame and embarrass people publicly.*

Altering the Pre-Provocation Mood

What we're doing in a given moment online alters our mood in such a way that it increases our likelihood of getting angry when provoked. One instance of this was found by Dr. Jenny Radesky and colleagues[64] who watched caregivers interact with their children at a fast-food restaurant. They found that the vast majority of caregivers used their phone during the meal, and when they were using their phone, they treated their children more harshly. Using technology in that moment essentially meant they had a shorter fuse and were more likely to react with anger.

In a much broader way, though, the information we consume online shifts the way we see the world. Thinking back to the discussion in chapter 5 about worldviews and lenses through which angry people interpret their experiences, those worldviews are often driven by the online content they consume. They develop their other-directed shoulds, their tendencies to jump to conclusions, their proneness to overgeneralize, and their catastrophic thoughts through the media they are exposed to. Since social-media feeds are often made up of content from others with similar values, users tend to live in an echo chamber, surrounded by people who agree with them. They lose valuable perspective and start to

---

* My students once shared with me that a relatively common way to get revenge on someone is to intentionally post an unflattering photo of them online. I collected some data on it and found that, indeed, 4 per cent of participants had done this. I wouldn't call that "common" but it's definitely happening. It also got me wondering how many unflattering photos have been taken of me when I'm teaching and shared by angry students.

believe that other people *should* see the world the way they do. They have a more difficult time empathizing or understanding people who see the world differently.

TIP

Social media lends itself to many of those angering thoughts described earlier (all-or-nothing thinking, labeling, other-directed shoulds). Take time to remember that the person you are interacting with is a human being with nuanced motivations who can't be summed up by a tweet or Facebook post.

Why is the Internet So Hostile?

When I first read the study by Fan et al. about the non-ignorable role of anger online, I had a million different thoughts. I wasn't surprised by the finding, so much as I wanted to know why this was the case. What is it about the internet, whether social media or just electronic communication, that lends itself to such anger and hostility? Why does anger spread so quickly? It's an interesting question and you can actually find some of the answers by comparing it to another angering and hostile activity… driving. There are elements of both activities, being online and being in the car, that tend to bring out anger.

Distance from the Person with Whom You're Engaging

When you are engaging with someone electronically, similarly to when you are on the road, you are distanced from them. You can't see the impact of what you are saying or doing on the person you are communicating with. This physical distancing makes it easier for people to express their anger in hostile or cruel ways. It is simply easier to say something hurtful when you are not looking the person in the eye when you say it.

Anonymity (or Perceived Anonymity)

Even when they aren't anonymous, people often report *feeling* anonymous when they are online (much like they do when they drive). In 2016, two researchers explored the impact of that anonymity on online interactions.[65] Participants worked with others to unscramble a series of words, believing they would get a prize if they did so successfully. The activity, however, was rigged so they would always lose and the others they were working with were part of the study and not actually other participants. When they were done, they were asked to write a blog post, assigned to either an anonymous or non-anonymous condition, about their experience in the study. The group that was anonymous was more hostile and aggressive toward their "partners" than the non-anonymous group.

What's moderately alarming about this is that people don't seem to realize how anonymity influences them. In a 2013 study I did on online ranting[66], 67 per cent of participants said they would rant online even if they weren't anonymous. They said being anonymous wouldn't change anything about how they behaved. The study above, though, suggests that isn't true and that anonymity does influence them whether they know it or not. There are likely a lot of people out there who fail to recognize how their behavior is influenced by this anonymity or perceived anonymity.*

Exacerbated Impulsivity

Much of what we consider to be anger problems might actually be impulsivity problems. What I mean is that lots of people are

---

* I can't help but think back to what Dr. Rosenthal (chapter 4) said regarding crowds existing in an online world. We know one of the reasons why people do things in groups that they might not do alone is because they feel a sense of anonymity when they are in a crowd. The same psychological principles that drive in-person mobs may drive online mobs.

angry but are able to control that anger. They don't say or do cruel things, not because they aren't thinking them or don't want to do them, but because they are able to stop themselves from acting on their impulses. Others, though, get mad and express that anger impulsively, doing or saying things they regret.

The nature of online platforms lend themselves to exacerbated impulsivity. In 2016, an article in *The Lancet Psychiatry* referred to online impulsivity as "a public health issue" and explained a number of ways that impulsivity was exacerbated in the online environment.[67] The highlighted anonymity was an issue, but the article also pointed to the absence of some controls that exist in the offline environment. The fear of consequences when offline (from police or other people in power like teachers or parents) are not as present online, so some hostile, cruel, or aggressive behaviors feel safer.

Rewards and Modeling

An unusual but important dynamic that occurs on social media is the way people are rewarded and encouraged for hostility. As evidenced by the Fan et al. study described earlier, anger spreads more quickly online than other emotions (so, for instance, angry tweets are more likely to be liked and retweeted than non-angry tweets). What this means to the person posting, then, is that their posts are most likely to be rewarded with likes and shares if they are angry or if they cause anger. It goes back to that basic behaviorism that we discussed in chapter 3. People emote in the ways they are rewarded for, so when they are rewarded for anger, hostility, and aggression, they keep doing it.

Of course, as was discussed in chapter 3, emotional expressions aren't completely informed by rewards and punishments. Modeling also plays a role. People do what they see others do, especially others of similar or higher status. So the already angry nature of social media tends to bring on more anger. The existence, too, of celebrities and politicians* using social media

---

* Can you think of any celebrities – or maybe even world leaders – who have a habit of taking to social media to express anger and hostility?

as a tool for anger, hostility, and cruelty models for people that this is an acceptable way to emote. Again, the hostility and anger that already exist online tends to drive even more hostility.

ANGER FACT

Survey respondents report being aggressive online approximately once per month on average.[68]

Strategies for Dealing with Anger Online

Much of what we've already discussed in this book remains relevant here. You should of course, for example, make sure you keep your goals in mind, stay calm, and ask if the anger is justified. In some ways these things are actually a little easier in the online environment because you usually have time to calm down and give some thought to your response. Whether you are dealing with a stranger or someone you know, there are, however, some specific things to consider when dealing with anger online. At the core of each of these, though, is the need to avoid adding additional fuel to the fire by bringing in your own anger.

Wait

I had a professor in college who never let students ask about a grade within 24 hours of getting the grade. She said she wanted the emotional response to the grade to dissipate before they had a conversation about it. I don't know that 24 hours is a magic number for this, but there's a good reason to take some time before responding. Remember, another person's anger at you will typically lead to emotionality from you (such as anger, anxiety, sadness, guilt). Taking some time before you respond will allow that emotion to dissipate and potentially help you clear your head. Much like what was brought up by Ephraim in chapter 5, this is one of the upsides of dealing with online anger rather than in person. There usually isn't a need to respond immediately so you are free to take some time and think through your response. Emotions are relatively short lived so waiting just 20 to 30 minutes might provide you with enough time to look at and think about things differently.

TIP

Waiting for your own emotions to dissipate can be a valuable strategy. Unlikely in in-person interactions, but online you will probably have time to decide if and how you want to respond.

Try Taking it Offline

I used to work at a shelter for adolescents and one of the first things we learned when it came to managing conflict was to remove the audience. The general feeling was that having other kids there watching the conflict made everything more complicated. The child in crisis might feel the need to save face, the other children might do things to intentionally encourage the conflict, and you the person trying to intervene might feel pressure to act a certain way. The same thing is true here. If you're on social media for this interaction, the audience of other users will likely make the situation more difficult.

Instead, try and connect in other ways (depending, of course, on your relationship with them). If the technology allows, direct message or email might be useful as it will remove the audience. You may also want to give them a call or schedule a time to talk. Given everything described above regarding how distance can exacerbate the hostility, maybe having an in-person conversation is a better option.

Avoid the Angry Emojis

One of the interesting things about online communication is how often people go out of their way to explicitly communicate their emotions (without just stating them). They feel the need to use ALL CAPS, angry faces, extra exclamation points, bold text, or a variety of other mechanisms to indicate that they are angry. Those approaches are not terribly compelling, though, if you're actually trying to change a person's mind or engage in a healthy conversation about something. They likely come across as superfluous and weaken the broader point you're trying to make. There's nothing wrong with telling someone you're angry in an email, but it's likely better to just say you are angry without the need to express it via a frowny face.

It's not that you should never use emoticons or emojis when you communicate. There's a time and place for them, particularly the positive ones. Emoticons and emojis can be used to lighten mood and to signal something emotional that is unclear from the text.* A smiley face, for instance, might make it clear something was a joke or was intended to be lighthearted (for example, "That's assuming I don't quit my job before then. :)"). A sad face might signal that you are feeling particularly down about something ("I can't go out tonight because I have an early morning meeting. :("). But they can also be used as a sort of passive-aggressive form of online communication where the author intends or pretends to lighten an aggressive comment with a smiley face or LOL ("Hopefully, you'll be on time for

---

* The origin of the emoticon reveals that it exists for exactly this purpose. When a joke was misunderstood on a message board at Carnegie Mellon University in 1982, one of the people involved in the online conversation, Scott E Fahlman, responded with "I propose the following character sequences for joke markers: :). Read it sideways." I blame him every time one of my kids sends me a string of 20+ emojis devoid of any context or meaning I can discern.

once. LOL"). Ultimately, be thoughtful about what emotions you try to express this way and how you choose to express them.

Have Someone Read Your Response Before You Send/Post It

Emotionality, especially anger, can often act as a lens by which people interpret the things they read. That means that the person you are responding to might misunderstand the intent of what you wrote because they were angry at the time they read it. It is similarly possible that your own emotionality, in response to their anger, might influence what you wrote in ways you don't realize. For both of these reasons, it's smart to have someone read what you wrote before you send it or post it. Getting another pair of fresh eyes on it prior to sending it can offer some much-needed perspective.

Ask Yourself Why You're Responding

To revisit something I talked about in chapter 6, think about your goals for this particular situation. What is it you are trying to accomplish with this response? Is what you're trying to accomplish a worthwhile or achievable goal? If not, what's a different goal you can have in this situation? If it is worthwhile and achievable, what's the best way to accomplish it? These are questions you should ask yourself before responding to online anger, because they should inform how you move forward. You should also remember that sometimes, maybe even often, choosing not to respond is a viable and reasonable option.

For many people, this is a challenge. They feel so compelled to respond because of that defensiveness or desire for revenge that they don't think clearly about what they really want from the interaction. Some goals might not be achievable (such as convincing an angry stranger on the internet that they are wrong about their politics). Even when goals are achievable,

---

* People sometimes ask me why I choose to argue with people on the internet when I know that I'll never change their mind. The answer is that I'm not really arguing with them and I'm certainly not intending to "win" the

accomplishing them requires a thoughtful and meaningful approach. It might require an offline conversation, time spent calming down before connecting again, or something else.

Staying in the Moment

One thing that has always struck me about online anger and hostility is how free people often feel to attack one another in ways I can't imagine they would in person. The things I have been called online are unlike anything I've ever experienced offline. That said, character assaults can look a lot of different ways. They aren't always overtly hostile or intentionally cruel. Sometimes, we insult people unintentionally by overgeneralizing or labeling them in more subtle ways. A conversation with a person who is angry ends up being about more than it should be because we have a hard time staying in the moment. In this next chapter, we'll talk about how to avoid character assaults when talking with an angry person.

argument. I'm trying to convince the people who might be reading along. I'm using it as an opportunity to share my ideas with people who might not be sure how they feel yet.

CHAPTER 13

STRATEGY EIGHT: AVOID CHARACTER ASSAULTS

"You're Doing the Thing You Always Do"

There's a scene in the 2019 movie *Booksmart* that I both love and hate. For those who haven't seen it, it's a comedy about two best friends who spend the evening trying to get to a party the night before their high-school graduation. They run into a host of problems as the night goes on and some things happen that put a strain on their friendship. Ultimately, they have an argument that starts over something relatively minor. One wants to leave the party and the other wants to stay. It quickly escalates, though, when one of them says "I'm not leaving because you're doing the thing you always do." At that point, the disagreement stops being about whether or not they leave the party and becomes about much more. The disagreement explodes into an all-out fight.

I hate this scene because it's so painful to watch. These are two lifelong best friends trying to enjoy what little time they have left together before going away to college. Watching them erupt at one another like this hurts. I love this scene, though, because it feels so realistic. It plays out exactly how I have seen and experienced arguments like this play out. They both stopped trying to resolve anything and started trying to score points with hurtful comments. "You're selfish and mean." "You're a fucking coward." "You're a bad friend."

Character Assaults Can Look a Lot of Different Ways

What I mean when I say you should avoid assaulting someone's character is that you should avoid saying hurtful things as an attack on who they are as people (calling them stupid, mean, a bad friend). On the surface, this seems easy. Obviously, if you're trying to have a productive conversation or healthy interaction with someone, you want to avoid insulting them. Frankly, even if you aren't trying to have a productive conversation and want to just be done with the interaction, it's still probably not a good idea to assault someone's character. It might feel good in the moment to some people but little good can actually come from such a character assault.

That said, it's pretty common for people to say or do something insulting when they are in these contentious situations with an angry person. There are two reasons why. First, people can get caught up in the emotion of the moment – perhaps they get angry themselves – and they lash out to make themselves feel better. Remember, anger can be thought of as an emotional desire to lash out, so it is completely natural to *want* to say or do something hurtful when angry. That instinct for revenge, the one we discussed in chapter 6, that you need to let go of in order to meet your goals, kicks in and you briefly want to hurt the person more than you want to resolve the disagreement.

The second thing that sometimes happens, and this one is less obvious, is that people don't necessarily realize they've attacked someone's character. Like the *Booksmart* example above, the offense is borne out of a tendency to generalize or label. When you watch the argument in *Booksmart* escalate, you can identify the exact moment things go wrong.* It's when one

---

* I'm not suggesting that one person is at fault and the other is innocent. Far from it. There was plenty of opportunity for either friend to de-escalate things. But that statement – the reference to what she "always" does – was the point that the argument stopped being about whether or not they should leave and started being about something else.

of them generalized beyond the context of the specific situation to make a comment about the person's broader personality with "you're doing the thing you always do." This tendency to generalize beyond the current situation to a broader personality characteristic is often why disagreements escalate into arguments or all-out fights. When someone is angry with you, it's easy to think or say things like, "You always do this," or "You can be so irrational when you're angry." When you do that, you're generalizing and labeling the person's behavior in such a way that it sounds and feels like an attack to them.

Honestly, even if it wasn't intended as an attack, it is one. When you generalize or label, you're taking a singular event and making it part of a pattern that is reflective of a broader problem. You're saying, *this thing you are doing right now that bothers me… it's a thing you do often and therefore is something I see as a character flaw.* The situation stops being about *what they did* and becomes about *who they are*.

For instance, imagine you make a mistake at work and one of your co-workers gets angry with you. They send you a hostile email that you find inappropriate and upsetting. You understand why they are angry and even take responsibility for the mistake you made, but you think they should have responded differently. You immediately fire an email back to them* that reads, "I don't appreciate how you responded to this. Your constant hostility to me is unfair and unprofessional."

Such a response might seem completely reasonable and even accurate. This hostility you're responding to might be way too frequent, unfair, and unprofessional. There might be an actual pattern of problematic behavior there that needs exploring at some point. It doesn't matter if it's true, though. It likely won't be productive in the moment for two reasons. First, that defensiveness we talked about in chapter 10 is more likely to come out when they are feeling attacked. Once the conversation becomes about *who they are* instead of *what they did*, you should expect them to get defensive, and that

---

* Because you hadn't yet read the chapter on dealing with anger online.

defensiveness makes it harder for them to think clearly to have a productive conversation. Second, the problem with generalizing like that is that you inadvertently let them off the hook. In this hypothetical example of the hostile email, which of these two sentences is easier for the other person to dispute?

1. "What you wrote was hostile and unprofessional."
2. "You are hostile and unprofessional."

The first one is quite a bit harder for them to dispute, right? It forces them to look at the singular thing they did – the email they wrote – and justify whether or not it was unprofessional or overly hostile. They have to defend that particular action. They may try and respond with, "How dare you call me unprofessional?" to which you can respond with, "I didn't. I said this email was unprofessional."

ANGER FACT

Overgeneralization opens the door to an escalation of anger and ushers in negative fallout.[69]

If you generalize and make the conversation about who they are as a person by asserting that they are hostile and unprofessional, they can easily point to examples to dispute it. Remember, as we learned in chapter 1, people's behavior is not terribly consistent across situations, so they will have a lifetime of non-hostile examples they can pull from to justify themselves as a kind and professional human being. They can likely easily point to times when they have not been hostile toward you or when they have been professional as evidence against your claim of "constant hostility."

But What if There is a Pattern?

At the same time, though, there are patterns of behavior from other people you may want to address. In the example above, maybe the person really is frequently – not *constantly*, but often – hostile and unprofessional via email and you don't want to ignore that issue. Maybe the person you're interacting with really does have a character flaw (maybe it's their anger) and you want to address it. How do you deal with that if it's not productive to talk to them about the pattern? Here are two approaches:

Addressing the Single Incident is a Start

Simply pointing out the single incident provides feedback that may help them see the broader pattern. A few years ago at work, a friend and co-worker sent me an email over a contentious issue. In an attempt to address the issue, I forwarded that email (copying my friend) to another administrator. When things were concluded, my friend wrote me and told me I had upset her by forwarding her email without her permission. She didn't say, "you always do this" or call me "insensitive" or "careless." She simply communicated that she didn't like that I had done that.

I bring it up for two reasons. First, I felt terrible. I hadn't intended to upset her. Frankly, I was completely unaware that she would be troubled by my having forwarded it on. She didn't want the email read by other people and I hadn't realized that. I don't think of myself as a careless person, but that was a careless error. Second, it forced me to think about whether this was a broader issue for me. Had I done this to others who hadn't brought it up to me? Was I regularly careless this way? I don't necessarily know the answers to those questions, but I do know that I pay more attention to it now than I used to. My friend letting me know that I upset her that one time led to a broader change in behavior for me going forward.

> **TIP**
>
> Focusing on a specific thing the person did or said instead of on a broader pattern can help the person hear the concern. It feels less like an attack.

Wait for a Less Emotional Time and Plan Ahead

The other way to address those broader patterns is to wait until you are no longer in the heat of an emotional moment to discuss it. As you well know by now, when people are angry they aren't always thinking clearly and rationally. Using this as the time to talk with them about a personality characteristic that bothers you probably won't be productive. It will lead to defensiveness and feel to them like it's a way for you to turn the problem back on them instead of taking responsibility.

Having that Difficult Conversation

Let's imagine, for instance, you want to talk with the angry co-worker, not just about this email, but about the broader problem of their anger at work and hostility toward you. Here are five steps you can take to try and make that conversation more productive:

Decide if You Should and Articulate Your Goals

The first thing to do is decide if you really should talk to them about this issue. Is it your place, for instance, to give them this feedback or should it be coming from someone else? Is this concern really about them or is it actually about you (perhaps another part of this problem is that you are being overly sensitive or are less comfortable with conflict than others)? You may come to the conclusion that, yes, this is an issue worth discussing, but before you have the conversation you should do the work of unpacking whether it is the right conversation to have. It might also be worth considering if a direct conversation is the best way to meet your goal. It might be that you decide this person isn't likely to change through such a conversation and you may need another approach.

TIP

Before you have a difficult conversation with someone, take time to articulate your goals to yourself. What does success look like to you? Is that obtainable?

Plan Ahead and Set Up a Time

You should decide on a time and plan ahead. Regarding the time, you may want to set something more official up with them. Let them know in advance that you've got something important you want to discuss with them and make sure that you give it enough time. Letting them know in advance helps send a message about the gravity of the situation and helps you ensure that you'll have enough time to communicate what you want to communicate. Related to that, give some thought to what you want to say and how you want to say it. What are the major points you want to get across? For instance, in the above example about email hostility, perhaps what you want to say is that you understood you made a mistake, that it's ok they were angry with you, but the way they communicated that anger was hurtful to you. Maybe you want to tell them that it's fine for them to call you on your errors but that you want them to be more careful and understanding of your feelings when they do so. Planning out the significant points you want to make in advance helps make sure you communicate what you think needs to be communicated.

Make the Health of the Relationship a Priority

When you meet, be understanding of their emotions and keep the health of the overall relationship in mind. As we've discussed throughout the book, the goal here shouldn't necessarily be to win an argument or to convince them they have wronged you. It's to get them to change their behavior – specifically their treatment of you – moving forward. That goal might not happen in this particular discussion, but it's even more unlikely to happen if you aren't respectful of their feelings when you meet. Do your best to be tactful and kind, and to pay attention to how you phrase things ("You're always so hostile" comes across very differently than "I've found many of your emails to me to be hostile").

Be Open to Feedback

In chapter 1, we talked about how people can somehow evoke particular types of responses from other people. We might unintentionally do something to actually bring out another person's hostility. I'm not suggesting that the other person's negative treatment of us is warranted or that we deserve abuse – far from it. What I'm suggesting is that we should be open to feedback regarding our role in these interactions. Disagreements like this are rarely the fault of a single person. As we have this difficult conversation, we should be willing to think about how we might need to adjust our approach moving forward as well. You should make a point of listening to them and giving some thought to that feedback.

Give Them Time

Finally, be sure to give them space and time to think about and reflect on what you're asking of them. In any contentious conversation, it's very unlikely that you'll find a resolution during the meeting. There may be hurt feelings, additional disagreement, and maybe even some anger during the conversation. Do your best to be patient with those feelings and disagreements and understand that even if the person agrees to make an effort to change their approach, that change may take some time.

It Won't Always Work

In a lot of ways, these guidelines assume a certain level of emotional maturity of the person you are interacting with. They assume the person wants to have productive conversations, that a person has similar goals to you, and that they have some ability to manage their feelings in emotionally charged situations. Those people do indeed exist. Even people who are prone to anger can be capable of having these sorts of goal-driven, productive conversations. However, there are of course angry people in our lives who are not going to be able to do this effectively, no matter how much thought or planning we put into it. Sometimes we have to acknowledge that we are only one side of this conversation and know when to let things go and to disengage. We come on to this in the next chapter.

CHAPTER 14

STRATEGY NINE: KNOW WHEN TO DISENGAGE

PRIORITIZING PHYSICAL SAFETY

Remember that learning how to deal with angry people is not about tolerating physical and emotional abuse. Always remove yourself to a safe space if you believe you are in danger.

Hard to Think About, Write About, or Act On

I want to preface the chapter with the following: This was by far the most difficult chapter to write. The decision to disengage from a toxic relationship is a really big thing to consider and it feels overwhelming to write about it or to offer suggestions for when or how to do it. On top of that, it's deeply nuanced, so everything I wrote felt incomplete. I kept saying to myself, "But what about those situations where…?" or "That might work if the person isn't…." And on top of all of that, I couldn't find many resources to help me write it. Most of the research out there is about emotionally or physically abusive relationships, usually with a romantic partner. Those are relevant, but not the same as what I'm trying to cover. I'm trying to help people figure out what to do when they have a relationship with an angry someone – any kind of relationship (such as friend, co-worker,

189

sibling, parent, spouse) – that is having a negative impact on their life and isn't improving. How do you know when to end that relationship? What does ending that relationship look like and how do you do it?

But then something occurred to me that helped me think through it. The struggle I was having writing this chapter likely mirrors the struggles we all have around abandoning toxic relationships. The nuance I was uncovering as I tried to organize my thoughts is part of the challenge. How important a decision it is along with all the potential consequences of that decision are what makes it hard to move forward. The lack of resources out there are likely because it's hard to think about, write about, or act on.

Yet people are struggling with this every day and tell me they need help. They don't know what to do. They have an angry person in their life who is making their life difficult and they don't know what to do about it. The good news is (going back to the beginning of the book where we talked about angry people vs. people who are angry) we can think about this topic two ways. Disengaging from one of those one-off incidents with an angry person vs. disengaging from a more long-term relationship with an angry person. We can use some of the same principles from the first to inform the second.

Two Examples

Let's start with two examples of people who have disengaged from angry people in very different ways. You'll see that disconnecting might look very differently, depending on the circumstances and nature of the relationship.

Alex

Take, for instance, Alex, who shared with me a story about a troubled relationship with her best friend from childhood. Alex was in her late 20s when we spoke and she told me that she had had the same best friend for almost 15 years. They had been very close through middle school and high school, but she acknowledged that her friend always had a serious anger problem that scared her and left her feeling emotionally exhausted. She described her friend as being easily triggered by everyday frustrations like long queues or things not working correctly. She told me that when her friend was mad, she would yell or swear or even hit things.

Alex wasn't usually the target of that anger, but it was sometimes directed at her in a way that made her feel sad or small. They had gone to different colleges but had stayed in touch and still lived in the same city. She told me that, at a certain point, she just felt like she had to break off contact. Getting together was just too exhausting for her. Her friend's anger had gotten worse over the years and she was starting to feel overwhelmed by it. She had tried to talk with her about it, but her friend just didn't see it as a problem and didn't seem to care about how it was affecting Alex.

Eventually, Alex decided she didn't want to have a relationship with her anymore. It was difficult for her because they shared some other friends, but that wasn't the bulk of the challenge. The real issue was her own guilt. She told me that even though she knew she was making the right choice, she felt guilty about it. Alex didn't have a conversation with her friend right away. At first, she just pulled back from spending time with her. She didn't go out with her as much and was less responsive to texts. She never reached out first. Eventually, though, her friend asked her if something was wrong, and so Alex told her how she was feeling. Predictably, her friend got mad and Alex felt guilty, but she stuck with it. They continued to text every now and then, but eventually that stopped too and they just drifted apart.

Charlie

Meanwhile, another person I spoke to opted to disengage from their angry person in a very different way. For Charlie, the angry person was intertwined much more deeply into his life. It was his dad. The situation was very similar to those cases I described early on in the book. Charlie's dad was easily angered and said cruel things when he was mad. He was never physically aggressive, but he was very hostile in a way that made Charlie uncomfortable.

At the time we spoke, Charlie was in his mid-40s and his dad was in his 70s. About five years before that, though, Charlie had decided to limit contact with his dad. A major factor here was that Charlie had young kids and he didn't want them to see and experience the kinds of things he had seen and experienced. Charlie had no reason to think his dad could or would change, so he decided he was going to spend less time with him, and that he would keep his kids away from him as much as possible.

Charlie didn't want to cut off all contact, though. He acknowledged that his dad was near the end of his life and was worried he might regret a decision to completely disengage. He kept wondering how he would feel if his dad died and he didn't have a chance to say goodbye. Instead, he spoke to his mom about it, shared his concerns, and told her he was going to limit contact between his family and his dad. He explained to her that he didn't want this to cause problems for his relationship with her, but that he understood this was going to make things more complicated.

His approach was really just to cut back on the time they spent together and to keep his kids away except for special occasions. When those occasions did happen, they never stayed very long. He continued to spend time with his mom, but she would usually come over without Charlie's dad. They talked on the phone every now and then, and they emailed somewhat regularly, but much of it was designed so that Charlie and his kids wouldn't be there if and when his dad blew up. Overall, Charlie was glad he made the change even though it had made things more complicated logistically. He also told me that it made the limited time he did spend with his dad more pleasant, because he wasn't as anxious. He used to constantly fear his dad's temper, but now he felt like he had put some things in place to prevent the kinds of problems those outbursts would cause.

Creating Boundaries with People Who Are Bad for Us

The interesting thing about this is that it's really easy, hypothetically, to justify disengaging from toxic people in your life. The people I talk with about this tell me all the time that we should create boundaries with people who are bad for us. People don't seem to have any trouble with that idea in the abstract. The problem comes, though, when it's time to actually try and cut someone out of their life. That's when the nuance, the practical barriers, and the emotions enter the picture. That is when people tell me they don't know when or how to do it. Sometimes they flat out tell me they can't disconnect because the angry person is so deeply entrenched in their life or other relationships (a co-worker, a boss, a family member, the parent of their child, and so on).

When to Disengage

There's no easy answer to this question of when we should disengage. It's considerably easier, though, when we're talking about one-off interactions that happen with strangers than when we're talking about long-term relationships. In these sorts of single-episode interactions with an angry person, I would suggest disengaging as soon as one of three things happens: (1) you no longer feel safe, (2) interacting with this person is not good for you, or (3) you realize that a resolution is unlikely or impossible. If you are worried about your safety, you should disengage immediately and get to safety. If you don't think the interaction has a chance of being productive any longer, you should find a way to end it and move on.

I think these same three guidelines can be applied to longer-term relationships too. It's time to disengage when you don't feel safe, when the relationship is no longer good for you, or when you realize that it will likely never improve. We should acknowledge first, though, that the details here obviously depend on the context of the relationship with the angry person. As I've mentioned throughout the book, angry people may be intertwined in our lives in ways that make disengaging exceedingly difficult. How you choose to relate to an angry boss is different from an angry spouse or an angry parent. Decisions about cutting off a friendship with a lifelong friend might be different than those involving a more recent acquaintance. There are many factors to consider here. Unlike most one-off interactions, there may be real consequences of disengaging that you have to factor in.

That said, it's also worth noting that disengaging doesn't necessarily mean cutting off all contact. It can look a lot of different ways. It *can* mean disengaging altogether and no longer being part of the person's life, but it can also mean spending less time together, interacting less often, or even limiting those interactions to specific ways of communicating or specific venues. Regardless, let's go through some things to consider as you decide what you want your relationship with this angry person to be like.

They are Emotionally or Physically Abusive

It's undeniable that another person's anger *can* lead to physical or emotional abuse. It doesn't usually, though. Anger is an exceedingly common emotion – experienced by most people a couple of times per week to a couple of times per day – and many people are able to handle their anger productively or even usefully.[70] That said, as we've discussed, the emotion itself involves a desire to lash out. Chronically angry people sometimes act on that desire and the people in their lives may suffer the physical and emotional consequences.

Physical abuse involves various forms of physical aggression including hitting, slapping, kicking, pulling hair, biting, or a variety of other ways of causing you physical harm (such as harming your loved ones, harming your pets, refusing to allow you to take your medication). Anger, along with other emotions such as jealousy or even fear, are clearly relevant but the abuse can also be motivated by a variety of other factors like a desire for power or control of the other person. The causes of physical abuse are typically broader than just their anger.

The same can be said for emotional abuse which includes them frequently insulting or criticizing you, keeping you from spending time with friends or loved ones, gaslighting you, finding ways to humiliate you, or attempting to control what you do, how you dress, who you spend time with, and more. Such patterns are, again, typically motivated by much more than anger.

Ending or leaving an abusive relationship is well beyond the scope of this book. There are a variety of barriers to those trying to leave such a relationship. For anyone who is the victim of abuse, I would urge you to get help from a professional by reaching out to an intimate partner violence resource.

TIP

If you believe you might be in an emotionally or physically abusive relationship, contact a professional for help. There is a resources section at the end of this book.

Spending Time with Them Feels Exhausting

I have talked to a number of people about what it's like to be in a relationship with an angry person, and they routinely tell me that it feels scary and emotionally draining to them. They are usually, though not always, talking about a particular type of angry person here – the type who tend to voice their anger outwardly or aggressively by yelling, screaming, or hitting things. They don't necessarily feel the threat themselves. They aren't necessarily scared that they will be harmed by the person. They are scared the person will hurt someone else, embarrass them, or just startle them with a moment of rage.

Because the other person's anger is scary to them, they find themselves actively working to prevent the person from getting mad. They spend all of this emotional energy trying to keep the person from exploding. They end up feeling like they can't be themselves because they are working so hard to manage the other person's emotions. That sort of effort is exhausting. People say they "walk on eggshells" to describe the general sense of discomfort and uncertainty they experience. They do the work of managing their own emotions not in a way that makes them feel good, but to protect the feelings of someone else. They take responsibility for someone else's feelings, and in the end they prioritize the feelings of the other person over their own.

If you get to a place with an angry person where being with them feels exhausting in this way, you might need to consider whether or not the relationship is worth staying in the way you are. There may be things you can do to manage those feelings, but if you've tried a variety of approaches, including things I've suggested so far, you may need to step away and see how it feels. This is especially true in those relationships where you've voiced your concern to them and they don't take it seriously or seem willing/able to change.

How to Disengage

Again, in theory disengaging from an unhealthy relationship is easy and straightforward. You may tell them directly you want to cut off contact, you may slowly disconnect from them over time, or you might even cut them off entirely with no explanation. In practice, though, there are a number of barriers to such disengagements. For some, those barriers are practical aspects related to how the person fits into their life (a parent, a sibling, a co-worker), but for others the barriers might be more personal. Some people may experience guilt over ending the relationship. Others may be in a situation where the relationship serves an important emotional purpose in their life and ending it might lead to some emptiness, especially at first.

Figure Out What the Barriers Are

The first step to ending a toxic relationship is to figure out what's been stopping you until now. Some people will say it was a lack of awareness. They didn't realize the relationship was unhealthy for them before but now they do. For others, the barrier is their own emotions about ending it. They feel guilty about cutting off the contact, scared of how the person may react, or even sad about the relationship ending. Other people identify some practical barriers to leaving. They may live with the person or share other friends with the person, making cutting off contact more challenging. Finally, some identify real discomfort with the conflict that might come from ending the relationship. It feels easier for them to stay in the relationship because disengaging will be uncomfortable. Whatever the barrier has been, it's important to identify it so you can work through it and find solutions.

ANGER FACT

Approximately one in five women and one in seven men have experienced severe physical violence from an intimate partner in their lifetime.[71]

Find Ways to Address these Barriers

Once you've identified these barriers, you can take steps to address them. If it's your feelings of guilt or sadness that are holding you back, make an effort to explore where those feelings are coming from and what you can do about them. Consider getting help from a professional therapist if it feels necessary. If the barriers are more practical, start working through some solutions. You may need to consider some relatively significant life changes to address those practical problems (if the angry person is your housemate, you may need to find a new place to live. If it's a sibling, you may need to address how you handle family gatherings going forward).

Know That it Doesn't Have to Be All or Nothing

Disengaging from an unhealthy relationship doesn't have to mean completely cutting a person out of your life. It doesn't necessarily mean you'll never see the person again. It could also just be cutting back significantly on contact with them. Instead of saying, "I'm done with this person," and never seeing them again, you might just make the intentional decision to spend less time with them or to interact with them less often.

This is important because the idea of disengaging from an angry person entirely can be scary or even impractical depending on who the person is in your life. Disengaging is about making a healthy decision on how much interaction you are going to have with that person. It should be based on a combination of factors, such as the toll those interactions are having on you and what you can practically manage given the person's role in your life.

Be Prepared to Deal with the Guilt

One of the most difficult parts of ending an unhealthy relationship is the guilt that sometimes follows. That guilt is normal and even healthy, and it doesn't necessarily mean you've done the wrong thing. Guilt is an emotion and, like any emotion, it serves an important purpose in your life. You feel guilt because it's one of the ways your brain communicates to you that you *may* have caused harm and then those guilty feelings motivate you to address that error. It helps motivate you to repair damage you may have caused in those cases when you actually have done something wrong.

TIP

Pay attention to the origin of that guilt you might be feeling. Is it rooted in real and reasonable expectations or are you expecting too much of yourself?

But just like anger (another emotion that signals there's a problem), it isn't always rooted in the reality of a situation. Just as those unreasonable other-directed shoulds might lead to anger, unreasonable self-directed shoulds might lead to guilt (I *should* put their needs before my own). It's quite possible this guilt is one of the things that's been preventing you from leaving this relationship. Be aware of that and plan for it. If you find yourself feeling guilty, try to assess whether that guilt is rooted in real responsibilities you are neglecting or unreasonable expectations you are putting on yourself.

It is also possible that the guilt isn't coming from your expectations but from what the other person has put on you. They consistently send the message that you *should* be there for them and you've internalized those expectations. The guilt you feel is the result of the unreasonable expectations they have of you to help manage their emotions.

TIP

It is hard to tell when you're being gaslit, as that's the entire nature of gaslighting. It's a complex manipulation tactic, but if you have concerns about it, you should seek help from a professional.

A Skill that Requires Practice and Thoughtfulness

The nine strategies, including the current one, that I've described for you so far don't happen on their own. In most circumstances, you can't expect to do just one thing and hope it resolves the situation. The experiences and interactions we have with angry people are emotionally and socially complicated. Navigating them means putting a variety of strategies together in nuanced ways. It means staying calm while you think about your goals, reflecting on the other person's anger and your response to it, dealing with people who don't necessarily want to deal with you, and more. Being successful at dealing with angry people is a skill that requires practice and thoughtfulness. Most importantly, it requires a desire to work through these situations in a healthy and positive way. In the next chapter, we'll discuss how to do build that desire and implement strategies together.

CHAPTER 15

STRATEGY TEN: USE THESE STRATEGIES TOGETHER

Cultivating an Identity

I want to end here by revisiting some of the things we started with. Dealing with angry people isn't just about having the tools available to you. It isn't just about knowing how to use those tools. It's about embracing an identity as someone who wants to interact with angry people productively and effectively. It's about having good, healthy, clear outcomes in mind when you interact with people. It's about trying to stick to those goals even when the other person gets angry.

Not everyone does that. In fact, if I had to guess, I would estimate that most people don't operate that way when they interact with angry people. They might embrace less useful goals of trying to get revenge or trying to prove they are in the right. They don't consider the situation from the other person's perspective. They don't try to come to a resolution and they fail to recognize some of the less obvious factors that might be influencing the other person's anger (including those things they themselves are bringing to the interaction).

To get around all that, you need to consider your own worldview and explore the lenses you might be looking at the world through. In chapter 5, we talked about the typical lenses of chronically angry people. How they have unreasonably high or unfair expectations of others, tend to dichotomize and think of the world in all-or-nothing ways, or how they tend to catastrophize the bad things that happen to them. Missing from that discussion, though, was how you also have schemas and worldviews that inform how you see the situations around you. You also have a set of lenses that might influence how you interact with people.

You may, in fact, have a very similar set of worldviews to the people you are interacting with. You may have similarly unreasonably high expectations of them that leave you feeling like they "shouldn't" be angry. You may tend to overgeneralize in ways that keep you from being able to fully distinguish what they are *feeling* from how they are *acting*. You may have a tendency to catastrophize that makes their anger feel worse to you than it otherwise would. The same patterns of thinking that influence their anger may influence your reaction to their anger.

There may, however, be some other lenses that drive these interactions. A tendency to engage in self-directed shoulds, for instance, might mean that you take on too much responsibility for the feelings of others. You may find yourself thinking things like, "I need to help calm them down" or "If I do that, they'll be mad at me." There's obviously nothing wrong with considering the feelings of others, but when it becomes overly taxing or exhausting for you, it's likely gone too far. Personalization, meanwhile, might mean that you make their anger about you in ways that it wasn't. You see their anger as reflective of your having made mistakes you didn't necessarily make. You catch yourself thinking, "They're mad because I screwed up again" and get down on yourself.

What this really means is that working effectively with angry people requires that you have done a certain amount of work to understand your own thoughts, feelings, and behaviors, especially as they relate to others. How they feel and express their anger is influenced in part by how you interact with them. How you interact with them is influenced in part by your identity and worldview. Do you see yourself as a calm person who can make effective choices in these emotional moments? Are you someone who at least wants to see the big picture in these situations and is making an effort to do so? Do you have a sense of where and when you are taking too much responsibility for their feelings? It's important to embrace such perspectives and be aware of yourself to be most successful in these situations.

Revisiting Those Five Caveats

When we started this book, I introduced five caveats about dealing with angry people I wanted you to consider throughout:

1. Their anger might sometimes be justified.
2. Anger can be both a state and a trait.
3. When people are angry with you, you likely get emotional too.
4. Angry people aren't necessarily monsters.
5. Angry people are sometimes toxic and dangerous.

I want to revisit these because so much of dealing with angry people is about remembering these five things. The strategies I've described in Part Two of this book really require that you consider each of these caveats. The reason you need to diagram a person's anger, for instance, is because it will help you determine if their anger is justified (even if their treatment of you was not justified). You need to find ways to stay calm because in these situations with angry people, you likely get emotional too. And even though angry people aren't necessarily "bad people" (though sometimes they might be), we may still need to disengage from them because they are bad for us.

Putting The Strategies Together

Let's go through some examples of how to integrate these strategies in the workplace and at home and see what they look like.

Anger at Work

Imagine, for instance, you are at work and you get an email from one of your co-workers that reads, "Hey, you really dropped the ball on this. I'm really upset and am going to need to talk with you about it later." You have a co-worker who thinks you mucked something up and is obviously angry with you.

As we talked about in chapter 12, situations involving email or other forms of online anger like this allows you to prepare in advance. You have the advantage of time because you got an email in advance of the actual conversation. Chances are, when you received the email and read it, you started to have your own emotional responses that might have included some anxiety, guilt, defensiveness, anger. In a moment like that, it's important to stop yourself and do a few things.

First, diagram the situation from their perspective and ask if the anger is justified. Ask yourself if you are really in error in this situation or if there's a misinterpretation from the other person. It's also important to determine, though, all the factors that might be contributing to their anger. Have they been under a lot of work stress lately that might be exacerbating their response to this? Did they misunderstand what actually happened in a way that made their anger worse? Are they catastrophizing the impact of your mistake? Is their anger being exacerbated by the people around them? Do their preconceived ideas about you or others involved in this situation inform how they are feeling right now? Use some of that time to develop some insight into the bigger picture to better understand where their anger is coming from.

Second, remain calm and think about your goals. In a situation like this, their anger at you, especially in the context of work which could have really negative consequences for you, is likely to lead to some intense emotions from you. Try to use strategies like deep breathing, grounding, or even a mantra to stay calm in that moment. Taking a moment to remind yourself "I can handle this" will feel empowering as you move into some consideration of your goals. You need to decide what the most important outcome is for this situation. This decision is likely rooted in that diagramming you already did. If you determine that you really did make a mistake, your goal may be to address it and try to put it right. But if you decide that this was not your mistake or that it is an overreaction from the other person, you may decide to address that issue instead.

Finally, you need to decide the best way to address that goal in this situation and avoid doing the things that run contrary to that goal. It sounds easy in theory, but it is challenging in practice when our own emotions often interfere. We get anxious, angry, or defensive, and we say or do things that run in opposition to what we actually want to accomplish. In a case like this, we may want to defend ourselves, try to blame someone else for the error, or even passively attack the other person's character ("You were late with a project just last month"). True or not, these approaches likely just interfere in the overall goal of solving the broader problem. Instead, work on identifying solutions to the specific problem or problems here and start down that path.

Anger in a Family

Of course, by now we know that the angry people in our lives present in all sorts of ways. We aren't always dealing with a one-off event like above. We need to handle those one-off events successfully, of course, but other sorts of angry people bring different problems. People in our lives may have deeper or more generalized anger problems. As we talked about in chapter 1, there are some with an angry personality who get angry often, express it in a variety of ways (usually outwardly), and often leave you feeling overwhelmed, anxious, or worse.

Imagine, for instance, you have an angry parent.* Like the case study in chapter 1 (Izzy), this parent seems like a different person when they are angry. They can be loving, supportive, and kind much of the time, but quickly become aggressive and cruel when they get mad. As with Izzy, this isn't necessarily a relationship you want to end. They are one of your parents, after all, and you have deep emotional and personal connections to them. And even if you did want to end that relationship, the practice of doing so might be logistically challenging because

---

* Many of the people I spoke to for this book told me that the angry person in their life was one or both of their parents. They also shared with me how hard it was for them to disengage from that relationship for both emotional and logistical reasons.

of other connections to that person (siblings, another parent, grandchildren).

At the same time, though, you can modify *how* you interact with that person. How often, where, what you talk about, who you are with – these are all elements that you have at least some control over. If you find yourself in a situation where you are needing to spend time with someone who is chronically angry, like at an upcoming family event, take some time to do the following in advance of the event and during.

Spend some time thinking about your goals and planning around those goals. What is it you hope to accomplish at this upcoming family event? Do you simply want to get through it without an argument? Do you want to avoid that conversation but not feel like you've sacrificed your feelings in the process? Do you want to have a tough but important conversation with the person? Do you want to avoid them altogether? Think through the different iterations of what you might want, and make some plans for how to accomplish them. Avoiding an argument is relatively easy if that's truly all you want, but avoiding an argument AND not feeling like you've sacrificed your feelings is considerably harder. By deciding what you want in advance, you can better figure out how to get there and be mindful about what you need to do in the moment.

Situations like these, whether it's with a parent or someone else you have a longstanding relationship with, bring with them a complex and nuanced set of dynamics. When there is a history with someone, the appraisal doesn't just include an evaluation of the particular moment. It includes an evaluation of your complicated history together. If someone on the street is angry with me, my reaction is based mainly on the information in front of me. But if a longtime acquaintance is angry with me, my response to that will be based on what kind of person I consider them, ways we have interacted before, the kind of relationship I want to have with them, and more. As you diagram the angry incident, think through those complex dynamics and consider how they might be impacting your appraisal.

Related to that, in chapter 8 we talked about how anger can look a lot of different ways. Not everyone yells, swears, or expresses their anger in an outward way like people expect them to. Others cry, pout, disengage, or channel it in other ways. This is true, not just of anger, but other emotions as well. When it comes to emotional expressions, people don't always behave in the way you expect them to. That means that what you think is anger might actually be something else, such as hurt, sadness, guilt, jealousy. More likely, though, is that the anger is actually a lot of different feelings mixed together. Emotions don't happen in a vacuum. People feel a lot of different things all at once. Again, as you are diagraming this anger, be sure to consider the different ways emotions can look.

Finally, when a parent (or anyone else we have a long-standing relationship with) gets angry with us, intentional or unintentional character assaults are easy and common. The longtime relationship you've had with them essentially means you have a lot of information to pull from when it comes to possible insults or generalizations. You can easily find evidence from their past to use against them. For all the reasons we talked about in chapter 13, it's important to avoid those sorts of assaults. They are typically unproductive, certainly, but they also have the potential to cause long-term or permanent damage to the relationship. Instead, try to keep the focus on the goals you outlined in the beginning.

Final Thought

There was something I thought about a lot as I was writing this book. It was relevant during that first chapter on the angry personality, especially as I think about what a personality really is. It's a concept I try to remember as a parent, as a teacher, and in any other role where people might look up to me. When all is said and done, a person's personality is really reflected by the choices they make. What they might think in a given moment doesn't matter nearly as much as what they do in that moment.

It doesn't matter how many times I tell my kids to eat healthy or exercise or to be kind to people, if they don't see me living those values in my day-to-day interactions they will quickly recognize that I don't really value them.

In the end, it sort of feels like our personalities are really made up of the little decisions we make in our day-to-day life. We are our choices.* That matters here because being successful at dealing with angry people often means embracing that as part of your personality. As I mentioned at the start of this chapter, dealing with angry people is about more than having a set of tools that you know how to use – it's about wanting to use them. It's about deciding that you want to be the kind of person who can manage the anger of others successfully. It's about recognizing that, when you are dealing with angry people, you aren't trying to score points or win arguments necessarily, you're trying to come out on the other side of that interaction with a positive outcome. Once you've decided that, it's about living that value in your daily life.

---

* That doesn't mean we can't have an off day sometimes or make *some* decisions that are inconsistent with our values. I'm allowed to value healthy eating and enjoy ice cream every now and then. I am similarly allowed to value kindness and caring for others, but sometimes slip or prioritize my own feelings.

FURTHER READING AND RESOURCES

USA

The National Domestic Violence Hotline:
www.thehotline.org
800-799-7233

UK

Refuge National Domestic Abuse Helpline:
www.nationaldahelpline.org.uk

Victim Support
www.victimsupport.org.uk

Women's Aid
www.womensaid.org.uk

Australia

www.1800respect.org.au/

REFERENCES

1   How Americans value public libraries in their communities. Pew Research Center, Washington D.C. www.pewresearch.org/internet/2013/12/11/libraries-in-communities/

2   Burd-Sharps, S., and Bistline, K. (2022, April 4). Reports of road rage shootings are on the rise. Everytown Research and Policy. www.everytownresearch.org/reports-of-road-rage-shootings-are-on-the-rise/

3   Meckler, L., and Strauss, V. (2021, October 26). Back to school has brought guns, fighting and acting out. *The Washington Post.* www.washingtonpost.com/education/2021/10/26/schools-violence-teachers-guns-fights/

4   www.mindyouranger.com/anger/anger-statistics/

5   www.thehotline.org

6   Martin, R. (2022). The Anger Project. www.alltheragescience.com

7   Vouloumanos, V. (2021, June 23). This psychology professor explained how to deal with people when they're angry with you, and it's something that everyone should know. www.buzzfeed.com/victoriavouloumanos/anger-researcher-explains-how-to-deal-with-angry-people

8   Dominauskaite, J. (2021, June). 6 useful tips on how to deal with angry people, according to psychology professor on TikTok. www.boredpanda.com/how-to-deal-with-angry-people-tiktok/

9   Martin, R. (2022). The Anger Project. www.alltheragescience.com

10   Allport, F.H., and Allport, G.W. (1921). Personality traits: Their classification and measurement. *Journal of Abnormal Psychology and Social Psychology*, 16, 6–40.

11   Allport, G.W., and Odbert, H.S. (1936). Trait-names: A psycho-lexical study. *Psychological Monographs*, 47(1), i–171.

12   Allport, G.W. (1961). *Pattern and Growth in Personality.* New York: Holt, Rinehart and Winston.

13   Buss, D.M. (1987). Selection, evocation, and manipulation. *Journal of Personality and Social Psychology*, 53, 1214–1221.

14 Cattell, R.B. (1949). The Sixteen Personality Factor Questionnaire (16PF). Institute for Personality and Ability Testing.

15 Costa, P.T., and McCrae, R.R. (1985). *The NEO Personality Inventory Manual.* Odessa, FL: Psychological Assessment Resources.

16 Deffenbacher, J.L., Oetting, E.R., Thwaites, G.A., Lynch, R.S., Baker, D.A., Stark, R.S., Thacker, S., and Eiswerth-Cox, L. (1996). State–trait anger theory and the utility of the trait anger scale. *Journal of Counseling Psychology*, 43(2), 131–148.

17 American Psychiatric Association. (2022). *Diagnostic and Statistical Manual of Mental Disorders* (5th ed. Text Revision).

18 Gene Environment Interaction. www.genome.gov/genetics-glossary/Gene-Environment-Interaction

19 Ferguson, C.J. (2010). Genetic contributions to antisocial personality and behavior: A meta-analytic review from an evolutionary perspective. *Journal of Social Psychology*, 150, 160–180.

20 Wang, X., Trivedi, R., Treiber, F., and Snieder, H. (2005). Genetic and environmental influences on anger expression, John Henryism, and stressful life events: The Georgia Cardiovascular Twin Study. *Psychosomatic Medicine*, 67(1), 16–23.

21 Stjepanović, D., Lorenzetti, V., Yücel, M., Hawi, Z., and Bellgrove, M.A. (2013). Human amygdala volume is predicted by common DNA variation in the stathmin and serotonin transporter genes. *Translational Psychiatry*, 3, e283.

22 Peper, J.S., Brouwer, R.M., Boomsma, D.I., Kahn, R.S., and Hulshoff Pol, H.E. (2007). Genetic influences on human brain structure: A review of brain imaging studies in twins. *Human Brain Mapping*, 28, 464–473.

23 Eisenegger, C., Haushofer, J., and Fehr, E. (2011). The role of testosterone in social interactions. *Trends in Cognitive Science*, 15, 263–271

24 Jeffcoate, W.J., Lincoln, N.B., Selby, C., and Herbert, M. (1986). Correlation between anxiety and serum prolactin in humans. *Journal of Psychosomatic Research*, 30, 217–222.

25 Panagiotidis, D., Clemens, B., Habel, U., Schneider, F., Schneider, I., Wagels, L., and Votinov, M. (2017). Exogenous testosterone

in a non-social provocation paradigm potentiates anger but not behavioral aggression. *European Neuropsychopharmacology: The Journal of the European College of Neuropsychopharmacology*, 27, 1172–1184.

26 Greenhill, C. (2020) Genetic analysis reveals role of testosterone levels in human disease. *National Reviews Endocrinology*, 16, 195.

27 Magid, K., Chatterton, R.T., Ahamed, F.U., and Bentley, G.R. (2018). Childhood ecology influences salivary testosterone, pubertal age and stature of Bangladeshi UK migrant men. *Nature Ecology & Evolution*, 2, 1146–1154.

28 Bandura, A., Ross, D., & Ross, S.A. (1961). Transmission of aggression through imitation of aggressive models. *Journal of Abnormal and Social Psychology*, 63(3), 575–582.

29 Van Tilburg, M.A.L., Unterberg, M.L., and Vingerhoets, A.J.J.M. (2002). Crying during adolescence: The role of gender, menarche, and empathy. *British Journal of Developmental Psychology*, 20(1), 77–87.

30 Bailey, C.A., Galicia, B.E., Salinas, K.Z., Briones, M., Hugo, S., Hunter, K., and Venta, A.C. (2020). Racial/ethnic and gender disparities in anger management therapy as a probation condition. *Law and Human Behavior*, 44(1), 88–96.

31 Marshburn, C.K., Cochran, K.J., Flynn, E., and Levine, L.J. (2020, November). Workplace anger costs women irrespective of race. *Frontiers in Psychology*, 11.

32 Salerno, J.M., Peter-Hagene, L.C., and Jay, A.C.V. (2019). Women and African Americans are less influential when they express anger during group decision making. *Group Processes & Intergroup Relations*, 22, 57–79.

33 Carstensen, L.L. (1991). Selectivity theory: Social activity in life-span context. *Annual Review of Gerontology and Geriatrics*, 11, 195–217.

34 Martin, R.C. (2010). Contagiousness of Anger (Unpublished raw data).

35 Martin, R. (2022). The Anger Project. www.alltheragescience.com

36 Dimberg, U., and Thunberg, M. (1998). Rapid facial reactions to emotional facial expressions. *Scandinavian Journal of Psychology*, 39, 39–45.

37 Schachter, S., and Singer, J. (1962). Cognitive, social, and physiological determinants of emotional state. *Psychological Review*, 69, 379–399.

38 Young, S.G., and Feltman, R. (2013). Red enhances the processing of facial expressions of anger. *Emotion*, 13, 380–384.

39 Zimmerman, A.G., and Ybarra, G.J. (2016). Online aggression: The influences of anonymity and social modeling. *Psychology Of Popular Media Culture*, 5, 181–193.

40 Stechemesser, A., Levermann, A., and Wenz, L. (2022). Temperature impacts on hate speech online: Evidence from 4 billion geolocated tweets from the USA. *The Lancet Planetary Health*, 6, 714–725.

41 Rosenthal, L. (2003). Mob Violence: Cultural-societal sources, instigators, group processes, and participants. In: Staub, E., *The Psychology of Good and Evil: Why Children, Adults, and Groups Help and Harm Others*. Cambridge: Cambridge University Press, 377–403

42 www.buzzfeednews.com/article/alisonvingiano/this-is-how-a-womans-offensive-tweet-became-the-worlds-top-s

43 www.ted.com/talks/jon_ronson_when_online_shaming_goes_too_far/transcript

44 Fan R., Zhao J., Chen Y., and Xu K. (2014). Anger is more influential than joy: Sentiment correlation in Weibo. *PLoS ONE*, 9, e110184.

45 www.ucl.ac.uk/pals/news/2017/nov/audience-members-hearts-beat-together-theatre

46 Schudel, M. (2021, November 3). Aaron Beck, psychiatrist who developed cognitive therapy, dies at 100. *The Washington Post*.

47 Beck, A.T. (1999). *Prisoners of Hate: The cognitive basis of anger, hostility, and violence*. New York: Harper Collins.

48 Martin, R.C., and Dahlen, E.R. (2007). The Angry Cognitions Scale: A new inventory for assessing cognitions in anger. *Journal of Rational-Emotive and Cognitive Behavior Therapy*, 25, 155–173.

49 Martin, R.C., and Vieaux, L.E. (2013). Angry thoughts and daily emotion logs: Validity of the Angry Cognitions Scale. *Journal of Rational-Emotive and Cognitive Behavior Therapy*, 29, 65–76.

50 de Quervain, D.J., Fischbacher, U., Treyer, V., Schellhammer, M., Schnyder, U., Buck, A., and Fehr, E. (2004). The neural basis of altruistic punishment. *Science*, 305, 1254–1258.

51 Carlsmith, K.M., Wilson, T D., and Gilbert, D.T. (2008). The paradoxical consequences of revenge. *Journal of Personality and Social Psychology*, 95, 1316–1324.

52 Martin, R. (2022). The Anger Project. www.alltheragescience.com

53 Zillmann, D., Katcher, A.H., and Milavsky, B. (1972). Excitation transfer from physical exercise to subsequent aggressive behavior. *Journal of Experimental Social Psychology*, 8, 247–259.

54 Martin, R. (2022). The Anger Project. www.alltheragescience.com

55 Spielberger, C.D. (1999). *State-Trait Anger Expression Inventory-2*. Odessa, FL: Psychological Assessment Resources.

56 Lazarus, C.N. (2012). Think sarcasm is funny? Think again. *Psychology Today Blog. Think Well.* www.psychologytoday.com/us/blog/think-well/201206/think-sarcasm-is-funny-think-again

57 Balsters, M.J.H., Krahmer, E.J., Swerts, M.G.J., and Vingerhoets, A.J.J.M. (2013). Emotional tears facilitate the recognition of sadness and the perceived need for social support. *Evolutionary Psychology*, 11.

58 Fabes, R.A., Eisenberg, N., Nyman, M., and Michealieu, Q. (1991). Young children's appraisals of others' spontaneous emotional reactions. *Developmental Psychology*, 27, 858–866.

59 Deffenbacher, J.L. (1996). Cognitive-behavioral approaches to anger reduction. In: Dobson, K.S., and Craig, K.D. (Eds.), *Advances in cognitive-behavioral therapy*. Thousand Oaks, CA: Sage, 31–62.

60 Adelman, L. and Dasgupta, N. (2019). Effect of threat and social identity on reactions to ingroup criticism: Defensiveness, openness, and a remedy. *Personality and Social Psychology Bulletin*, 45, 740–753.

61 Martin, R. (2022). The Anger Project. www.alltheragescience.com

62 Fan R., Zhao J., Chen Y., and Xu K. (2014). Anger is more influential than joy: Sentiment correlation in Weibo. *PLoS ONE*, 9, e110184.

63 Berger, J., and Milkman, K.L. (2012). What makes online content viral? *Journal of Marketing Research*, 49(2), 192–205.

64 Radesky, J.S., Kistin, C.J., Zuckerman, B., Nitzberg, K., Gross, J., Kaplan-Sanoff, M., Augustyn, M., and Silverstein, M. (2014). Patterns of mobile device use by caregivers and children during meals in fast food restaurants. *Pediatrics*, 133(4), e843–e849.

65 Zimmerman, A.G., & Ybarra, G.J. (2016). Online aggression: The influences of anonymity and social modeling. *Psychology Of Popular Media Culture*, 5, 181–193.

66 Martin, R.C., Coyier, K.R., Van Sistine, L.M., and Schroeder, K.L. (2013) Anger on the internet: The perceived value of rant-sites. *Cyberpsychology, Behavior, and Social Networking*, 16, 119–122.

67 Aboujaoude, E., and Starcevic, V. (2016). The rise of online impulsivity: A public health issue. *The Lancet Psychiatry*, 3, 1014–1015.

68 Martin, R. (2022). The Anger Project. www.alltheragescience.com

69 Martin, R.C., and Vieaux, L.E. (2013). Angry thoughts and daily emotion logs: Validity of the Angry Cognitions Scale. *Journal of Rational-Emotive and Cognitive Behavior Therapy*, 29, 65–76.

70 Martin, R. (2022). The Anger Project. www.alltheragescience.com

71 CDC. www.cdc.gov/violenceprevention/intimatepartnerviolence/fastfact.html

ACKNOWLEDGEMENTS

I am once again deeply indebted to family, friends, coworkers, and even some strangers who offered love, support, and insights as I worked on this book.

As always, I owe much to my family. I have a brilliant, talented, funny, and kind partner in my wife, Tina. She has been exceedingly supportive as I have worked on this book and it is a far better final product thanks to her insights. Together, we have two wonderful children, Rhys and Tobin, who are a constant source of joy, humor, and inspiration. As I said in the dedication, they make every day better. My mom, Sandy, has been a constant inspiration to me and many others. Sadly, my father passed away just a few weeks before my last book came out so I wasn't able to share that joy with him. I take comfort, though, in knowing that he would have been proud of me for both that book and this one. I have three incredible siblings, each of them with wonderful families of their own who I love dearly, and my wife's family is similarly important to me. I owe them all a great deal of gratitude for their support of my work.

I'm similarly blessed to be surrounded by amazing friends and coworkers, who inspire me with their talents, humor, and great ideas. I have been lucky enough to have many deep and meaningful friendships, including those from as far back as high school. Their support means the world to me. I also work with amazing people at the University of Wisconsin-Green Bay. Day in and day out I am surrounded by talented teachers, brilliant scholars, and hard-working and skilled students. You simply can't work in a place like this without benefiting from the wisdom of the people around you. I'm thankful for each and every one of them, and know that their influence has made this book a better work.

Over the last few years, I've connected with hundreds of thousands of people over social media, especially through TikTok and Instagram. I had no idea when I joined those platforms how rewarding it would be. While I love that there are so many people who are interested in my work, what I love even more is how much I've learned form them. Their stories and ideas have inspired me and this book has benefited so very much from their willingness to share their thoughts and experiences with me.

I am as always indebted to me to the wonderful team at Watkins Publishing, especially my editor Fiona Robertson, who has been so supportive as I wrote this book (and was patient with me when it took longer than I had hoped), and my publicist Laura Whitaker-Jones, who is a constant source of positivity and good ideas. I so appreciate their work along with everyone else at Watkins who helped make this a reality.

Finally, like so much of my work, I owe the great many scholars who study anger and other related topics. Their steadfast efforts to better understand these important human experiences is critical to helping people have healthier emotional lives. They are owed a significant debt of gratitude not just from me, but from everyone who seeks emotional wellness.